Published in the United States of America by
ABCKO Enterprises, LLC • Copyright © 2010 • All Rights Reserved.

ISBN/EAN13: 1451538502/ 9781451538502
Page Count: 166
Binding Type: US Trade Paper
Trim Size: 6" x 9"
Language: English
Color: Black and White
Related Categories: College / Golf / Recruiting

First Edition

www.ACollegeGolfPlan.com

Dedicated to Bill,
Kyle, Kelsi, & Connor

Without your love and support,
this journey would not have been possible!

A COLLEGE GOLF PLAN

"Realize Your Dream of Playing College Golf"

Amy Bodin

Published by ABCKO Enterprises, LLC

Table of Contents

Table of Contents

Introduction

So, your teen bounds into the room and announces he/she wants nothing more than to play golf in college, and, of course, he feels he has the talents for a top-notch Division I school! You shudder, act supportive, and wonder in the back of your mind – how are we ever going to do this…. can he/she really get a golf scholarship….. where do we start….. who do we call….. how do we get him noticed…. what is the process? You race to the internet; to the bookstore; talk to other parents; talk to counselors; contact recruiters; to begin your search. It becomes apparent that this is a complicated, confusing process with no step-by-step "how to" manual, particularly for the unique world of *college golf recruiting*. We know, we've been there!

We have gone through the experience of hiring/firing recruiters, researching every internet site and book we could find, talking to parents, coaches, tournament directors and more. It becomes extremely frustrating and confusing to know where to turn and how to get the ball rolling, when there is nothing out there specifically designed for the junior golfer. Through countless hours of research, interviews, pitfalls, false starts, and disappointments, we developed a systematic approach to navigate our way through the myriad of confusion. With our new insights, knowledge, and experience, we began helping other junior golfers, and their parents, with their search for the right college and the right college golf team. Many, many times we were asked to develop a manual by parents and junior golfers. And, so this book was born.

Being recruited for a college golf team is a very unique process set apart from other sports. The answers can't always be found in generically written recruiting materials, which are commonly directed towards the higher profile big team environment. High school and college golf is an individual sport with a team experience. It is much more complicated than your average team sport. In comparison to other teams, college golf teams are very small, and rarely have the recruiting budget of other large collegiate sports.

College golf coaches are looking for that exceptional individual who can compete independently and simultaneously, as a strong team member, with the formidable character exclusive to golfers. And, unless your junior golfer is one of those exceptions to the rule, college coach's won't find you, you will have to find them; and you will have to start early.

A College Golf Plan is designed to lead you out of the clouds of confusion and onto an easy-to-follow path to realize your junior golfer's dream of playing collegiate golf. We take you on an in-depth exploration of what steps to take to present the ultimate student-athlete package to college golf coaches, and into the perfect college for your junior golfer. A College Golf Plan answers how to build a college list, how to design a golf resume, cover letter, and swing video, how and when to market yourself, what to do when visiting a college and coach, when and how to apply to colleges, how to manage your time, and so much more. Take a moment to preview our **"Table of Contents,"** where you'll quickly find the ideal outline to answer all of your questions.

Best of all, A College Golf Plan is written from an experienced parent's perspective, with the junior golfer and their parents in mind. We help you navigate your student-athlete through the complicated college golf recruiting process with insights from other parents, college golfers, junior golfers, tour directors, university personnel, and college coaches; without the bias of a coach's or recruiter's mindset. This is the perfect tool to jump start your junior golfer's dream of playing college golf.

For the Parents

We know first hand the emotional and physical roller coaster that goes along with raising children, particularly teenagers. It's mentally and physically exhausting, yet, at the same time, the most rewarding experience ever. Walking the fine line of parental emotional balance is a challenge like no other. As if the every day isn't demanding enough, throw in a complicated schedule of high end travel sports (and maybe two or three sports with more than one child), and patience becomes stretched.

However, this is the time where you and your teen have to pull together to achieve the dream. Take a deep breath, and collaborate on a plan of action. As the parent of a junior golfer, you have likely already spent an enormous amount of time bonding with your teen during road trips to/from tournaments; before, during, and after tournaments celebrating or consoling (or both); strategically planning the right tournaments at the right time, etc. So, for the parent of a junior golfer, in particular, the leap to collaborate on a plan of action is more like a small hop, as you've been doing it all along. There hasn't been a coach or group planning your steps for you, you and your teen have had to go it alone. This experience is very unique from the team sports arena and is absolutely invaluable as you begin your next chapter.

We have heard every realm of advice as to the ideal parental role in helping your teen through the long and arduous road of athletic recruiting. Our best advice, from our experience, is that it is up to you. You, and you alone, know your teen best; you know their personality, their capabilities, their strengths, and their weaknesses. More than likely, you will take on the role of guide and supporter during this journey, with a healthy handful of assisting in the every day mundane tasks. There will be plenty of tongue biting, jaw clenching moments where you, as the adult, have to keep your cool and remember you are the guide.

Keep in mind that while all this turmoil is swirling around you, you are also preparing your son/daughter to go it alone for, probably, the first time in their life. As part of this process, you may need to nudge them to be the driving force through it all. With those gentle nudges (ok – so sometimes it's more like a hard push) that only a parent can give, you will have to remind them to send, follow up, fix their grammar, read it again, call, interact, ask questions, be mature, dress appropriately, watch their behavior, talk to their counselor, stay on top of their grades and so much more.

And, similarly, you will have to do the same thing – coaches are not only watching the student-athlete, they are watching the parents too. They are paying close attention to how you interact with your son/daughter on the course, after the tournament and during a college visit. It is just as important for you to conduct yourself in a suitable manner, as it is for your son/daughter.

We wish you the best of luck on your adventure, and hope that we are able to help you along the rocky road of college golf recruiting.

www.ACollegeGolfPlan.com

Chapter 1

The Four Year
High School Plan

The next four years are vitally important. They are your planning time for your next step in life, college. Becoming a college athlete can be a very long and arduous process. We lay out a step-by-step plan for you to follow throughout your high school years to realize your dream of playing college golf. These pages are your launching point; read, and follow them carefully. For areas that require a lot more attention, we've elaborated in the subsequent chapters. *All* of this information is essential to coordinating a solid college golf plan and will likely, get you where you want to be, even if you're unsure of exactly where that is right now.

There are no guarantees but, if you start planning early and execute at the right times, you have an excellent chance of playing college golf. There are hundreds, if not thousands, of college golf openings each year, and there are plenty of coaches who would love to have you on their team. Above all, keep an open mind. Most junior golfers seem to start out with a dream school or two and often end up many miles away from that dream school and, commonly, are happier with their final decision! Stay open to all possibilities, a different Division than you initially thought, a school further away than you originally considered, a smaller or larger school than you were planning on; there are hundreds of teams out there, all looking to fill spots – stay objective in your search.

The highly ranked schools avidly recruit the top 50-100 nationally ranked golfers early on. If you are not recruited (without effort on your part), then it is time to begin constructing a plan of action. You need to be proactive in your search and communication to coaches. Coaches are very busy coaching their own teams, traveling, staying abreast of Division rules, recruiting, etc. If you are not in the top coveted group, they need to hear from you – and they want to hear from you. As much as you don't want to miss an opportunity with them, is as much as they don't want to let a good, talented golfer slip through their fingers.

Coaches are under tremendous pressure to maintain a winning team, recruit the best players, and stay abreast of all of the guidelines and more. Recruiting is becoming more and more competitive and the race for a college coach to land that one "special" player has started earlier and earlier. The very talented player, but not "top" ranked player, feels left out in the dust and confused. There is an enormous advantage to being a very talented, but not "top" ranked player; once all the dust has settled, and the highly ranked schools have acquired their coveted players, it becomes your turn and there are still **plenty** of spots left at fantastic schools (sometimes even at those highly ranked schools).

FOUR YEAR HIGH SCHOOL QUICK OVERVIEW

Freshman Year
- ✗ Begin building a solid GPA.
- ✗ Join your high school golf team.
- ✗ Begin playing higher level golf tournaments.

Sophomore Year
- ✗ Keep up your grades – a good GPA is critical.
- ✗ Familiarize yourself with your high school and NCAA graduation requirements.
- ✗ Take the practice PSAT.
- ✗ Play in high school and high level golf tournaments.
- ✓ Begin researching and visiting colleges. ☐
- ✓ Gather your academic and golf reference letters. ☐

Junior Year
- ✗ Keep your grades up!
- ✗ Register at the NCAA Eligibility Center.
- ✗ Make sure you are on target with your high school and NCAA graduation requirements.
- ✓ Send your resume, cover letter, swing video, and golf references to college coaches.
- ✗ Take the PSAT, SAT, and ACT (twice, if necessary).
- ✗ Play in high school and national level golf tournaments.
- ✓ Strategically plan your summer tournaments carefully.
- ✓ Build relationships with college coaches and keep them informed on new information.
- ✓ Visit colleges and contact coaches to schedule interviews.
- ✓ Narrow your college list.
- ✓ Follow up, follow up, follow up.

Senior Year
- ✓ Keep your grades up – it's still important!
- ✓ Apply to colleges and send academic references.
- ✓ Research financial aid options.
- ✓ Accept "official" visit offers from college coaches and continue visiting colleges.
- ✓ Stay on top of your communications with college coaches' – be diligent.
- ✓ Make your final decision and sign The National Letter of Intent!

www.ACollegeGolfPlan.com

Freshman Year

Academics

* Start building a solid GPA. One of the most important elements for college acceptance (even within Athletics) is a good GPA. It is vitally important to begin now and keep your grades up. The truth is that by the time you begin applying to colleges, it is your GPA only through your junior year of high school that counts (you will begin applying to colleges in the fall of your senior year). It is these first three years of high school that matter most when building a strong GPA.

* Find out what kind of student you are. Many high schools place a lot of emphasis on Advanced Placement and Honors courses, and students feel pressure to take these courses. If you feel you can benefit from Advanced Placement courses, take an AP or PreAP class in a course you feel advanced in – if you are only able to achieve low Bs, Cs or Ds; then, more than likely, the AP route is not in your best interest. The nationwide collegiate standard looks at your base 4.0 GPA, and if a heavy load of AP classes is pulling your GPA down, then this is not your preferred plan of action. It is better to have a solid GPA than an assemblage of AP courses with grades in the 70s.

* However, one to four AP classes over your four years of school does look good and may give you the edge you need. By your junior year, you will know which class(es), if any, you are comfortable taking as an AP course(s) – go ahead and take an AP course or two your junior and senior year.

* Most colleges are looking for a strong GPA with some advanced courses. These classes don't necessarily have to be AP courses. You can be a year ahead in math, or take an extra math and/or an extra science, or you can take an Honors course, or you can test out of a "regular" class by taking an AP exam at the end, or you can take a class or two at a Community College. These are

all excellent ways to show you are "advanced" in your academics.

• Load up on "required electives" (these are usually Fine Arts, Foreign Language, Speech, Health, Technology Applications, Physical Education). Try and get most of these out of the way your freshman and sophomore years.

• Utilize tutoring to help with your classes. Many schools offer free afternoon tutoring sessions, or ask a teacher for their help, or to point you in the right direction.

• Get to know your high school requirements. Most high schools have a chart of requirements for graduation. The following is a good high school baseline for most college acceptance requirements, but always check with your high school:

Curriculum Subject Areas:	Credits
English/Language Arts	4 Credits
Mathematics	3-4 Credits
Science	3-4 Credits
Social Studies	4 Credits
Physical Education	1.5 Credits**
Health	.5 Credits
Technology Application	1 Credit
Foreign Language	2-3 Credits*
Fine Arts	1 Credit
Speech (Communications)	.5 Credits
Electives	3.5-5.5 Credits
Total Credits	25-28 Credits

*Some colleges may require 3 years of Foreign Language, check with the colleges of your choice.

Volunteer Work:

Do some volunteer work each year. It's important for colleges to see a diverse, well rounded person. Check with your high school, community/neighborhood, and church for a variety of volunteer opportunities.

FRESHMAN YEAR

Golf

- Download a copy of the "NCAA Guide for the College-Bound Student-Athlete" at www.ncaastudent.org. This guide is an excellent overview of the requirements to play NCAA collegiate golf. See our section on **"Know the Governing Organizations"** for further information.

- Try out for the high school golf team. High school coaches often hold try outs before the school year, so check their schedule during the summer. Call or email the coach or the school.

- Become a solid member of your high school team and begin building a rapport with your high school coach and teammates.

- If you haven't done so already, start playing in junior tournaments in your area. There are usually junior PGA tours in most cities, which conduct well organized local tournaments. Try playing in one or two intra/inter-state, and/or nationally recognized tournaments such as the AJGA or other tour groups, to get a feel for this level of tournament experience. See our section on **"The Junior Golf World and Its Importance"** for more detailed information.

- The ultimate high school goal is to play in nationwide tournaments. For the most part, college coaches tend to use the nationally ranked tournaments and/or state tournaments as their recruiting base point. However, a progression from Jr. PGA (or other local tour groups) to intra/inter-state tours to AJGA and other national tournaments is best; each time raising your ability, level of play, and player status (this isn't to say that testing the waters in national tournaments each year isn't a good idea – it is).

- The best place to find junior golf tours and tournaments is on the *Junior Golf Scoreboard* website. They have the best searchable list for juniors and they list just about every junior tournament in the nation. You can find them at www.njgs.com or www.juniorgolfscoreboard.com. See our section on **"The**

Junior Golf World and Its Importance" for more detailed information.

* Play practice rounds at courses before tournaments. Most courses offer a significantly reduced rate practice round prior to junior tournaments. Assess how a practice round affects your play in the tournament. You may be fatigued playing a full 18 holes the day before your tournament; or, when playing your practice round, you may find hitting multiple shots per hole benefits you, etc. Use this time to not only practice, but find your own personal practice round system that works best for you.

* Take lessons from a teaching professional and build a relationship with that teaching professional. If you don't have a teaching pro, ask your high school coach, and/or other junior golfers, or their parents for their recommendations.

* Begin keeping track of all of your tournaments to build a solid resume. You will need a good, strong golf resume to send to college coaches by the end of your sophomore year to the middle of your junior year. At this point keep track of *all* of your tournaments; you will narrow them down later when refining your final resume. ***Do not wait*** to do this from memory later. Keep track of:

  ‣ The course name, town & state
  ‣ The course yardage, slope, and rating which you played at that specific tournament;
  ‣ The tour/tournament name you played in;
  ‣ Your scores for each day and overall combined score;
  ‣ Your finish out of the total number of players in the field;
  ‣ The weather conditions;
  ‣ Any special information (such as making a cut, qualifying for another higher level tournament, player's field level, strong nationally ranked field, etc.);
  ‣ Any specific notes about the tournament to jog your memory later.

FRESHMAN YEAR

It is important to begin establishing an official handicap. Some junior tour organizations supply you with a GHIN number, as a member of their tour. If you belong to a country club, they can also establish a GHIN number for you. It is advantageous to have a tour establish your GHIN, as the tour posts official tournaments directly to the USGA GHIN. You are responsible for entering all of your other tournaments on the GHIN website. Be honest and enter **ALL** of your tournaments, good and bad. Go to www.ghin.com for further information.

Behavior:
It is essential to conduct yourself in a respectful manner at all times both on and off the course. College coaches watch, listen, talk to other coaches, and check on your behavioral background.

Sophomore Year

Academics

- Continue building your GPA and getting good grades. This is a crucial part of college evaluations. Having a sound GPA makes a college coach's job easier and may give you an edge during a coach's review of your qualifications.

- Have a meeting with your high school counselor to confirm you are on track for credits and courses. Also, discuss your intention on playing an NCAA sport in college to ensure you are on par to graduate on time with your class with all of the necessary NCAA and high school requirements.

- The following is an example of the NCAA Division I and Division II Core Course requirements. Remember these are only the "core" course requirements, not the total requirements for high school graduation:

Division I (16 Core Courses)	Division II (thru 7/31/2013) (14 Core Courses)	Division II (after 8/1/2013) (16 Core Courses)
4 Years of English	3 Years of English	3 Years of English
3 Years of Math (Algebra I or Higher)	2 Years of Math (Algebra I or Higher)	2 Years of Math (Algebra I or Higher)
2 Years of Science (1 Year of Lab Science)	2 Years of Science (1 Year of Lab Science)	2 Years of Science (1 Year of Lab Science)
2 Years of Social Studies	2 Years of Social Studies	2 Years of Social Studies
1 Year of Additional English, Math or Science	2 Years of Additional English, Math or Science	3 Years of Additional English, Math or Science
4 Years of Additional Core courses (can include Foreign Language)	3 Years of Additional Core courses (can include Foreign Language)	4 Years of Additional Core courses (can include Foreign Language)

SOPHOMORE YEAR

- Finish your "required electives" (these are usually Fine Arts, Foreign Language, Speech, Health, Technology Application, Physical Education). Try and get most of these out of the way your freshman and sophomore years. Use your junior and senior year to take your optional electives in courses that appeal to you. Test different areas, which you find interesting; this will develop a good sense of a possible college major.

- Sign up for the sophomore PSAT. The PSAT is the practice SAT and is a required standardized test your junior year. The PSAT is designed similarly to the SAT, giving you a solid example of the SAT. Taking the PSAT your sophomore year is excellent practice for the junior year exam. Your sophomore year scores are only an indicator of where you may score on the subsequent PSAT and SAT your junior year; they are not recorded scores. You can register for the PSAT through your school; check with your counselor.

- Take prep courses for the PSAT. The best place to find information on this is through your counselor or college career center. There are many organizations which offer prep courses; speak to your counselor about which are the best and most cost effective classes.

- Begin a search for colleges – the best place to search for colleges is www.collegeboard.com. This site offers excellent overviews of colleges in the U.S. See our section on "**Choosing the Right College(s) for You**" for further information.

Volunteer Work:

Do some volunteer work each year. It's important for colleges to see a diverse, well rounded person.

References:

Begin asking for reference letters from a teacher(s). You may have a teacher, counselor, or administrator who is "special" to you. Ask for their reference letter *now* because you never know if they will be at your school the following year.

Golf

This summer and the following summer are the most important two summers to get your name known in the junior golf world. Start exploring national tournaments such as AJGA, Optimist, Jr. Am Qualifiers, Jr. PGA Qualifiers, Jr. World Qualifiers and more!

- If you haven't done so already, go to www.ncaastudent.org and download a copy of the "NCAA Guide for the College-Bound Student-Athlete." This guide is an excellent overview of the requirements to play NCAA collegiate golf. See our section on **"Know the Governing Organizations"** for further information.

- Continue with your high school golf team and building your status as a solid member and leader of the team.

  - Ask your high school coach to sit down with you and develop a plan of tournaments (outside of your high school tournaments) to participate in over the spring and summer.
  - Talk to your coach about your college goals and get him/her involved in your college search.
  - Also, speak to your coach about Captain or Co-Captain responsibilities during your junior and/or senior years.

- Begin playing in as many higher level tournaments as possible. College coaches regularly scan "national" tournaments to locate talented players. Getting your name on one of the national boards is extremely important to playing college golf. This is an important golf summer and by now, you should be playing in the inter/intra-state tours, AJGA, and other national tournaments (if you are comfortable with national level tournaments, at this point). See our sections on **"Marketing Yourself"** and **"The Junior Golf World and Its Importance"** for further information.

TIP   Never withdraw from a tournament on your second day due to poor performance on the first day. This is a sure fire way to negate a coach's interest. The day after a poor round is your chance to prove yourself.

- In the spring, the AJGA typically offers pre-season tournaments for those who've not played in the AJGA before. They also offer courses on how to understand the AJGA system. Go to www.ajga.org to find out more information, and sign up to be on their email list to receive regular updates. See our section on "**The Junior Golf World and Its Importance**" for further information.

- Play practice rounds at courses before tournaments. Most courses offer a significantly reduced rate practice round prior to junior tournaments. The AJGA has its own practice round on the Monday before each tournament, as do other higher level tournaments. Continue assessing your best practice round strategy.

- Look into playing in junior amateur qualifiers such as the US JuniorAm Qualifier, US Amateur Public Links (www.usga.org), Optimist Qualifier (www.optimistgolf.org), etc. See our section on "**The Junior Golf World and Its Importance**" for further information.

- Continue lessons from a teaching professional. This is the time to get serious about improving your swing and your short game. Seek diverse teaching pros to work on different areas of your game.

- At this point, pull together a brief golf resume. You may have incomplete information (i.e. SAT & ACT scores, ranking, etc.) but that is okay – coaches understand. However, having a resume available when you visit a coach is a perfect way to become memorable and gives the coach ready made documentation to begin a file on you.

- Start visiting colleges. Plan "unofficial" visits around your travel golf tournaments (*an unofficial visit is a visit at your expense*). See our section on "**Visiting Colleges**" for complete details about the following list.

▶ Make a list of colleges that are near your upcoming tournaments. Even if these colleges are not necessarily schools you think you may be interested in – visit them anyway. You will be surprised how your decision changes over time. These visits also give you an early idea of the types of schools you may like and what is important to you in a college atmosphere.

▶ Schedule an on-campus guided tour (the guided tour gives some of the best information about the college and its programs). You can find information on tour times from the college website and/or by calling the school directly.

▶ Ask a lot of questions, take notes and pictures of the school and listen carefully. You will want to refer to this information later. After many visits to colleges, they tend to blur together and it is often difficult to remember the specifics.

• Although your sophomore year is a bit early to have any serious in-depth conversations with college golf coaches, you may want to consider meeting with the golf coach while on campus. During your sophomore year, college coaches cannot contact you off campus except through questionnaires and camp brochures. However, you can contact the college coach to schedule a time with him/her prior to your campus visit. Do not pop into his/her office unannounced.

According to NCAA Division I regulations: College coaches may *not* contact you in person, or by telephone, off their campus, until July 1 (or June 15 for Division II) after your junior year. They may ONLY send you questionnaires and camp brochures beginning your freshman and sophomore years; and may send you printed recruiting materials beginning September 1 of your junior year.

SOPHOMORE YEAR

Behavior:

It is essential to conduct yourself in a respectful manner at all times both on and off the course. College coaches watch, listen, talk to other coaches, and check on your behavioral background.

Begin building a "college file" with references, resume information, possible colleges, coach's information, etc.

Junior Year

This is your most important year both athletically and academically! This is the time to pull it all together and get out there marketing yourself!

Academics

- Essentially this is the last year you have to get that GPA in great shape. Work extremely hard this year to get/keep your grades up!

- When applying to schools, it is your GPA, through the end of your junior year, which colleges' review. They will ask for your first semester senior grades and what courses you are taking your senior year, but the "final" GPA they look at ends your junior year.

- Typically, high school counselors are required to conduct a "junior review" this year to ensure you are on track for credits and courses for graduation. If you do not receive a review date from your counselor, check with him/her to make certain this meeting happens. Don't forget to review the NCAA requirements with him/her.

- Take the PSAT, SATs, and ACTs:

  ▶ Take the PSAT during the fall. Normally high school's schedule this test for all juniors. Check with your counselor for the date, time, and location of the test.

  ▶ Take both the SAT and ACT tests, and take them more than once. These are essential tests, which colleges depend upon when making an informed decision on a student.

  ▶ Some colleges rely more heavily on either the SAT or the ACT – it is important to take both tests.

  ▶ Try to schedule two sessions of each test to be completed by early June of your junior year.

  ▶ Sign up for prep courses for the SAT and ACT. Research different prep courses and enlist the help of your counselor and/or college career center.

JUNIOR YEAR

> ▶ Your scores on these two tests may not only determine your acceptance into a school, but also an academic scholarship, and the size of that academic scholarship.

* To sign up for the SAT, go to www.collegeboard.com. To sign up for the ACT, go to www.actstudent.org.

* Really delve into your search for colleges, based on your interests, academics, and testing scores (go ahead and reach a little at this stage, but also remain on the realistic side). See our section on **"Choosing the Right College(s) for You"** for more in depth information.

> ▶ Search online and and/or send away for literature from colleges. Collegeboard.com is the best place to begin.
> ▶ Make a solid list and don't limit yourself to NCAA Division status, school size, location, public versus private schools or finances. These elements will come into play later as you narrow down your search (and after visiting schools); remain very open when creating your initial list.
> ▶ Seek assistance in building your list and pulling together your college golf plan.
> ▶ Ask your high school for an unofficial transcript at the end of your junior year. They may not have junior transcripts ready over the summer (seniors are their priority). You may have to piece meal it together a bit. At bare minimum, request an unofficial transcript through your first semester and your final semester report card of your junior year. You will absolutely want to have this information on hand if you are offered an athletic scholarship from a college coach.

Volunteer Work:
Do some volunteer work each year. It's important for colleges to see a diverse, well-rounded person. Check with your high school, community/neighborhood, and church for a variety of volunteer opportunities.

References:

Have a couple of solid academic reference letters from teachers, counselors, and/or administrators at this point. See our section on **"Applying to Colleges"** to learn more about when to use your academic references.

JUNIOR YEAR

Golf

This summer is your most important golf summer. Play in national tournaments such as AJGA, Optimist, Jr. Am Qualifiers, Jr. PGA Qualifiers, Jr. World Qualifiers and more!

- By now, you should be a prominent asset and leader on your high school golf team.

  - Ask your high school coach to sit down with you and make a plan of tournaments (outside of your high school tournaments), to participate in over the spring and summer.
  - Work hard to get you and your team to regional and state levels. College coaches take notice of state tournaments and are often impressed by regional performance.
  - Talk to your coach about your college goals and get him/her involved in your college search.
  - Also, speak to your coach about Captain or Co-Captain responsibilities for your junior and/or senior years, if you haven't already reached that level.

- At this point, researching and playing in nationally ranked tournaments should be part of your regular golf repertoire. College coaches are very busy and rely heavily on tournament information. They regularly scan "national" tournaments to locate skilled players. Getting your name on the national boards is extremely important to playing quality college golf. See our section on **"The Junior Golf World and Its Importance"** for more detailed information.

- Begin strategically planning your golf schedule for the upcoming summer. Look for AJGA tournaments, Junior Amateur qualifiers and nationally recognized tournaments such as the Junior PGA Championship, Junior Am, and Junior World. Accept offers to play in invitational's, even if they are not at a nationally ranked level. These are still strong tournaments, and show you are a desired junior golfer who can play against a tough field. Strategically planning this summer for maximum exposure is vitally important. The more national experience you have, the stronger your golf resume. See our sections on **"The Junior Golf World and Its Importance"** for more information.

* As we've said, the summer after your junior year is your *most* important golf summer. Know your capabilities and *really* do your research on different tournaments where you have the best opportunities to stand out amongst the crowd. Unfortunately, college coaches really do care about your ranking, so strategically placing yourself in the "right" tournaments is critical.

* College coaches attend national tournaments to evaluate players. There is usually a board announcing which coaches are there for the day. This is a wonderful way to be noticed. They are unable speak to you (check the NCAA guidelines), but you will definitely know who they are and when they are watching you – this is your time to shine. See our section on **"Marketing Yourself"** for further information.

* Play practice rounds at courses before tournaments. Most national tournaments have their own practice round(s) before each tournament.

* Continue lessons with your teaching professional. Seek different teaching pros to work on different areas of your game. Having a swing coach and short game coach, at this point, is important to the development of your game.

* Register at the **NCAA Eligibility Center** at the beginning of your junior year. This is an important element if you plan to play collegiate golf in the NCAA. You must prove your amateur status, your high school graduation timeline, your high school transcripts, and your SAT and ACT results. Follow the instructions at www.eligibilitycenter.org to complete the required information. Their site is very self-explanatory. Additionally, college coaches will need your NCAA Eligibility ID number in order to schedule an "official" visit later. See our section on **"Know the Governing Organizations"** for more detailed information.

JUNIOR YEAR

- Begin to market yourself. Thoroughly review our section on **"Marketing Yourself,"** to develop a complete plan for marketing your information to coaches.

  ▹ Complete your golf resume and cover letter, and begin sending them to college coaches. Be concise and original, and let coaches know your upcoming schedule – this is essential to a college coach. See our section on **"All About Resumes, Letters and Swing Videos."**

  ▹ Complete a golf swing video – strategically plan when to send this to coaches. See our sections on **"All About Resumes, Letters and Swing Videos"** for further information on developing a swing video and timing your communications.

  ▹ Follow up on your communications with coaches. Keep them informed on your upcoming schedule, and any new news you have, such as tournament scores, grades, test scores, etc. They want to hear from you. Coaches are extremely busy and you need to be proactive and diligent about staying on top of your communications, even if they do not respond.

- Narrow down your list of the colleges you are interested in and begin visiting them. See our section on **"Choosing The Right College(s) for You"** and **"Visiting Colleges"** for more in depth information.

  ▹ During your junior year, you should be scheduling unofficial visits at colleges on your list and arranging time with the college golf coach while on campus.

  ▹ **Do not** go unannounced to visit a college coach. Contact the coach prior to your visit and schedule time with him/her. Often times, the coach can organize a solid visit for you including a guided tour, time with the admissions office, visiting a professor, etc., in addition to time discussing their golf program.

  ▹ Make sure you are composed, well spoken, and well dressed on all campus and coach visits.

  ▹ Be prepared with a list of questions and a good attitude on your visits. Listen carefully, take notes, and pay attention.

▸ See our section on **"Visiting Colleges"** for more in depth information on meeting with a coach and planning a complete visit.

▸ **ALWAYS** send a thank you to a coach after a visit. Be professional and courteous.

Coaches can contact you via phone, after July 1 for NCAA Division I, and after June 15 for NCAA Division II, of your junior year. Watch for that communication and follow up.

References:

Have a couple of solid golf reference letters from coaches and teaching professionals. Additionally, have at least one "special" golf reference letter from another junior golf parent or junior tour official – this goes a long way in showing who you are, and the impression you make on others in the junior golf world. See our section on **"Marketing Yourself"** to learn more about when to use your golf references.

Behavior:

It is essential to conduct yourself in a respectful manner at all times both on and off the course. College coaches watch, listen, talk to other coaches, and check on your behavioral background.

> We can't emphasize enough how important your junior year is both athletically and academically; and it is your biggest marketing year. Make sure you have everything pulled together well, and start early getting your information into the hands of college coaches.
>
> On the next page is a brief timeline to follow through your junior year, based on the preceding descriptions. Use this timeline, the above descriptions, and the subsequent chapters to guide you through your junior year.

JUNIOR YEAR

JUNIOR YEAR QUICK OVERVIEW

September – December of your Junior Year

✓ Register at the NCAA Eligibility Center.

✓ Have a meeting with your high school counselor to make sure you are on track to meet the NCAA core course requirements and your high school graduation requirements.

✓ Complete your golf resume, cover letter, and swing video.

✓ Gather your academic and golf reference letters.

✓ Take the PSAT, SAT, and ACT.

✓ Play in your high school tournaments and other national junior tournaments.

✓ Pull together a good, narrowed list of potential colleges.

✓ Send your resume and cover letter early December, if you feel this is the best timing for you.

January – March of your Junior Year

✓ Send your resume and cover letter to your list of coaches – do not delay on this!!!

✓ Retake the SAT and ACT, and know your GPA.

✓ Begin planning your summer tournament schedule.

✓ Build relationships with coaches and communicate your upcoming schedule – respond to them immediately.

✓ Keep coaches informed on new information.

April – August of your Junior Year

✓ Send your swing video & summer schedule to coaches in April/May.

✓ Keep coaches updated and continue building relationships.

✓ Double check your upcoming schedule for maximum exposure.

✓ Visit colleges & contact coaches to schedule on campus meetings.

✓ Gather your golf reference letters and send them.

✓ Follow up with coaches – even with those who haven't responded to you. Stay in touch!!

✓ This is often the time when coaches extend verbal offers.

✓ If you don't have an offer you are happy with by August, and no prospects, follow up with the coaches' you've been working with and resend your information to your list of colleges. Also, consider sending to new colleges.

Senior Year

This is your time – the year you've been waiting for! Work hard this year marketing to coaches, visiting colleges and applying to colleges. Before you know it, you will be signing the National Letter of Intent!

September – November of your Senior Year

Thoroughly review our section on "Marketing Yourself" and "Applying to Colleges" for a complete description of the following processes:

* Begin applying to universities – check deadline dates for applications and scholarships. The best place to find this information is on the school's website. If you've received an "official visit" offer, the coach will likely help guide you through applying to his/her school prior to the visit (official visits are campus visits partially or fully paid for by an institution). See our section on **"Applying to Colleges"** for detailed information on the application process.

* Keep your grades up – they are still important to colleges your senior year. Colleges and coaches consider the courses you've chosen for your senior year and your first semester grades.

* This is the last opportunity for you to receive an offer for the early signing period, which is in November. See our section on **"Offers, Finances and Signings"** for further information.

According to NCAA Division I and II rules: A prospective student-athlete may make official visits beginning the opening day of their senior year. They can make one official visit per college, up to a maximum of five visits to separate colleges. Prior to an official visit, a prospective student-athlete is required to provide the college with a copy of their SAT, ACT or PLAN scores, NCAA Eligibility Center ID number, and Division I requires a copy of the prospective student-athlete's high school transcript.

The NCAA National Letter of Intent early signing period for golf usually begins the second Wednesday in November and runs for eight days. The regular National Letter of Intent signing period usually begins in mid-April and runs to early August. Check www.nationalletter.org for the exact dates.

- Follow up with coaches by sending your reference letters, swing video, and any other information they may need.

- Keep coaches regularly informed on new information. They want to hear from you and they won't forget you, if they receive regular updates. Coaches receive hundreds, if not thousands, of resumes – regularly staying in touch is absolutely essential!

- If you are offered an athletic scholarship from a college coach, you will need to decide whether to "verbally" accept or not before the November signing. A verbal acceptance is not binding and can be declined by either party (although it is not often retracted from a college coach, unless there is some sort of violation). See our section on "**Offers, Signings and Finances**" for detailed information on offers.

- If you decide to sign with a school during the November early signing period, remember this is a binding agreement. There are penalties for not attending the institution you sign with. See our section on "**Offers, Signings and Finances**" for further information on signings and offers.

- If you sign, make sure this is what you want – ***don't settle*** – there are plenty of coaches who don't get the student-athlete's they plan on, and new openings happen all of the time after the November signing through to the spring/summer signing. Review the questions we've presented at the end of this section before signing a National Letter of Intent.

- Keep up with your high school and other junior golf tournaments. Continuing to improve athletically is what this is all about!

December – April of your Senior Year

Thoroughly review our section on "Marketing Yourself" for a complete description of the following processes:

- If you didn't sign with a school in November or receive a verbal offer – **DON'T PANIC** – more often than not this turns out to be for the best!

- Many, many college coaches do not get their picks on the first signing. Commonly, student-athletes accept a verbal offer, but change their mind before the early signing.

- After the completion of the early signing period, you may hear from college coaches' who you had been working with previously. If you are still interested, act immediately and pursue these schools.

- At this point, reevaluate schools you liked that didn't extend you an offer. Check with those coaches to see where they stand on their signees and recruiting process.

- In early December, once the dust has settled from the November signing period, refine and resend your resume, a new cover letter, and your swing video, letting coaches' know you are still interested and available. Consider sending to new schools, which you hadn't worked with previously. Starting from square one may serve you well, and shed new light on schools you never thought of before.

- You may want to open yourself up to different divisions. If you were hoping for Division I, still pursue Division I schools, but open yourself up to Division II, Division III, NAIA and NJCAA (two year schools) schools.

- Follow the same procedures for communications, visits, and offers we previously described. Be diligent in following up and communicating with college coaches.

SENIOR YEAR

- Accept offers for official visits and keep an open mind. Official visits are a good sign of a coach's interest, and are typically very detailed visits. See our section on "**Visiting Colleges**" for further information.

- **ALWAYS** send a thank you to a coach after a visit. Be professional and courteous.

- Follow up, follow up, follow up!

The NCAA National Letter of Intent regular signing period usually begins in mid-April and runs to early August. Check their website at www.nationalletter.org for the exact dates.

May – August of your Senior Year

- If you don't sign in April, keep at it. Send out new updated information, visit new schools and follow up.

- Schools still sign up until the last date possible, which is usually around August 1.

- Keep up with your junior golf tournaments. There are plenty of tournaments for 18 year olds. Continue to improve athletically.

If you still don't sign with a school by August 1, then contact coaches about their walk on and try out policies. Many college coaches hold a walk on try out at the beginning of the school year. Some have open try outs, and others hold invitation-only try outs. More than likely, if you make the team as a walk on, you will not be offered a scholarship. However, work hard and prove yourself, and you could earn a scholarship down the road. If you don't make the team, consider Intramural or Club golf at your college, and make yourself known to the coach.

Questions To Ask Yourself Before You Sign

Signing a National Letter of Intent is a binding agreement and you **must be sure**. A few questions to ask yourself before you sign are:

▸ **Are you proud to say I attend XYZ University?**
You will know if you are settling if you aren't proud of your university and shouting it from the rooftops. Take some time to really visualize yourself at that university, with the team, and with the coach.

▸ **Are you comfortable with the size and educational offerings at the college?**
If this is not the school size you are really comfortable in, or it doesn't offer the major you would like, then this is not the place for you. You should get a good idea of these aspects when you are visiting the school. If it feels too cramped or too overwhelming, then you need to keep looking to find the right feel and educational offerings for you.

▸ **Are you comfortable with the coach and team members?**
These ten to fifteen people are your new family for the next four years. Make certain you are comfortable with them and can see yourself working and living with them, over the years.

▸ **Are you comfortable with the level of golf this team projects?**
If they don't have the same level of golf life style and attitude you do, then this is not the school for you. You may want to see more or less dedication, organization, commitment, and drive – if it's not right on par with who you are and what you are looking for, then keep going on your pursuit.

QUESTIONS TO ASK YOURSELF

▶ ***Do you feel you are on par academically and can keep your grades up in this environment?***
If you feel you may really be reaching to maintain a good solid GPA at this school, it is more than likely not for you. College is a huge adjustment from high school and much more demanding. When you compound this transition with the additional pressure of traveling on a collegiate sport's team, it becomes even more stressful. Most college teams pride themselves on their team's GPA, which adds another level of demands on you. Make sure your academic abilities are a good fit.

▶ ***Does this school have the look and feel for you?***
This may sound a bit intangible, but it is what your first impression of a school is always about. If it's not what you envisioned; too small, too large, too spread out, too cramped together, too modern, too old, etc., then this is not where you'll be comfortable.

Chapter 2

The Junior Golf World and Its Importance

Participating in junior golf tournaments is a key element to advancing your golf potential. While practice and lessons play an extremely vital role in developing your golf game, there is nothing like an organized golf tournament to truly, learn about the rules and pressures of competitive golf. Taking a step-by-step approach to advancing from one level of tournament play to the next is the best way to *really* learn about competitive golf. Each tournament, and new tournament level, helps you become a better golfer, an honest athlete, a controlled and sportsmanlike competitor, understand the rules to competitive golf, understand the junior field of golfers and so much more. By the time you reach national and international golf tournaments, you will have gained the knowledge base to compete at this level, effectively advance to college golf, and further.

The national/international tournaments are where you gain the best exposure to the collegiate golf world. This is where college coaches focus most of their recruiting efforts and time. How you advance to the stage of playing national/international level tournaments is a valuable learning process and requires a systematic approach.

Navigating your way through the myriad of junior golf tournaments can be confusing. And, if your intention is to play on a college team, you feel the pressure to move up and perform. As hard as it may be, relax and plan your strategy for the three summers during your high school years. Know your capabilities and don't over reach too early – this could prove disastrous and put you in a ranking position, which is difficult to recover from. Of course you need to stretch yourself in order to grow and move forward, but don't jump by leaps and bounds when you are not ready.

Talk to other junior golfers, their parents, tour directors, golf club pros, and/or seek consulting advice to find the best progression of tournaments in your area. Lay out a plan for where you want to be at the beginning and end of each summer. Be flexible, but keep your goal forefront at all times that you are trying to maximize your exposure to college coaches.

As we mentioned earlier, the absolute best place to begin your search is on the Junior Golf Scoreboard website at www.njgs.com or www.juniorgolfscoreboard.com, which lists just about every junior golf tournament in the nation. You are able to search by state, age, gender, month and more.

While high school golf plays an important role in your learning process, college coaches don't regularly focus their attention on high school tournaments unless they are at a regional and/or state level. That being said, being a member of a high school golf team is an important part of your growth and development.

TIP   **Never withdraw from a tournament on your second day due to poor performance on the first day. This is a sure fire way to negate a coach's interest. The day after a poor round is your chance to prove yourself.**

THE ROLE OF HIGH SCHOOL GOLF

Often high school golf gets a bad wrap because it is devalued in the college recruiting process, until you reach regional and/or state levels. This is a shame, because the education received on a high school team is invaluable and carries through to college.

It is likely that until entering high school and making a high school golf team, you have never played golf in a team situation before. As we all know, golf is an extremely individual sport and, up until your high school years, your tournaments have been focused solely on an individual level. The idea of a golf "team" environment was probably not in your vocabulary. Being a valued member of a golf team offers new insights to the college golf world, which can't be learned elsewhere, and practicing together as a team and embracing "team spirit" is new and exciting.

This will be your first time reporting to a coach on a daily basis and following a coach's rules and timeline. Having the experience of a high school coach's rules is advantageous to understanding the college golf coach and team. College coaches often take their coaching rules and timeline to the next level.

You may have heard (or are involved with, if you are already on a high school team) how high school tournaments are run, and which players on a team are asked to attend certain tournaments, but you've never experienced the process. Like college golf coaches, high school coaches typically send their top five players to compete in high school varsity tournaments. The best four scores are posted for that school's team (the highest score being dropped) to formulate a team's overall total score. At the same time, each individual score is posted and calculated to signify the individual final rankings for the tournament.

So, while you are competing to win individually, you are also competing to win as a team, while simultaneously competing against your own teammates. An individual can win a high school tournament while their team places fourth. On other team sports, either the team wins as a team, or they lose as a team. Team golf is very unique to other team sports in this way; it is both individual and team oriented, while also being extremely competitive amongst the team itself.

As we mentioned earlier, high school golf coaches often run their qualifiers much like college coaches. For the first time, you will be required to compete against teammates to earn your spot in that coveted "top five." Coaches may have slightly different approaches to qualifiers, but, in general, the team competes amongst themselves, and the lowest five scorers are sent to the varsity tournaments. Qualifiers may be on a per tournament or per season basis. Some coaches also have rules regarding a previous tournament finish, such as the low man/woman at the previous tournament is exempt from the qualifier for the next tournament. Whatever a coach's particular rules, both high school and college coaches utilize a similar systematic approach to qualifiers. This type of qualifying experience cannot be obtained anywhere else (even at non-high school tournament qualifiers).

As your high school years progress, discovering where you fit in on the team is an essential part of your growth. You may learn you are a leader; you have the ability to lead a group of individuals through the team experience while still maintaining their/your individual goals and status. Assessing your role in a high school team environment plays an important part of realizing where you may fit on a college team.

Learning to balance individual competitiveness, team spirit, sportsmanlike conduct towards the field AND your own teammates, are indispensable lessons which translate over to college golf, the business world, and overall relationships. Being on a high school golf team affords you a unique and invaluable experience which can't be found anywhere else in junior golf – experience which *directly* translates to college golf.

A WORD ABOUT SUMMER GOLF CAMPS

Many, many colleges and golf organizations hold excellent week-long (or more) golf camps over the summer. Several coaches have mentioned that they often find some of their best team members at these camps.

Summer golf camps are a great way to hone your skills in a dedicated week-long golf environment. However, we have found these camps to be a better teaching atmosphere in your younger years, before you reach the national junior playing field. Additionally, it becomes extremely difficult to schedule a golf camp amidst your demanding summer tournament schedule during your latter high school years.

That being said, if there is a college you are extremely interested in, it may be worth your while to invest a week at their summer golf camp to show your capabilities in a unique atmosphere, away from the competitive junior golf world. There are NCAA guidelines associated with recruiting and summer camps. You will want to review the rules prior to signing up for a camp, particularly if you are attending a camp in your latter high school years with the intention of being noticed. As with everything else, there are different levels of camps that you'll need to research to find which one best suits your needs and skill level.

JUNIOR GOLF TOURNAMENTS

If you are reading this book, it is likely that you have already ventured into the world of junior golf tournaments. Progressing from one step to the next, in junior tour organizations, is key to a junior golfer's development. Beginning at local level tournaments and working your way to national/international tournaments is the best approach.

If you haven't begun playing in competitive junior golf tournaments, we feel the best place to begin is with local, one day tournaments. The junior PGA offers a number of sections in different states. Commonly, the different junior PGA sections offer a series of one day (9 hole) summer tournaments beginning as young as age 6; and one or two day (18 hole) summer/winter tournaments through to age 18. They are very well run and reasonably priced tournaments. Young junior golfers learn a great deal about the game of competitive golf at these local tournaments. Visit www.pga.com/pgaofamerica/sections/ to locate PGA sections in your area.

Another place to look for local one or two day tournaments is with your city or town recreational centers. There are often a series of one day city tournaments sponsored by your local area. Ask other junior golfers, their parents, other tournament directors, or local golf clubs to recommend city junior tournaments.

When you're ready to move to the next level, an inter/intra-state two day tournament series is your next step. These summer series often exist within your state or a group of states, and are a more serious level of play. The inter/intra-state tours often require travel, are more expensive, and adhere to stricter PGA rules than the local area tournaments. These tour groups typically offer a stepping stone into national tournaments by providing ways to earn exemptions or qualify for national tournaments. Again, ask other junior golfers, their parents, tour directors, and local golf clubs for recommendations.

The ultimate goal of the junior golfer is to play in national tournaments. These tournaments are where college coaches spend a great deal of their summer recruiting time looking for talented junior golfers.

By the summer after your sophomore year, and especially the summer after your junior year, you should be playing in a well strategized list of national level tournaments. Really take time to plan your tournaments for the summers after your sophomore and junior years to maximize your exposure to college coaches.

Assess your tournament abilities before planning your summer season. Know where you stand against the field(s) and what your best approach is to national level tournaments. It is important to strategically place yourself in the best tournaments for your ability level.

While national/international tournaments are the best avenue to attain college coaches' attention, certain tournaments may not be the best fit for your skill level, and you may very well send the wrong message by competing in an environment above or below your talent level. There are a number of national/international tournaments all around the country, comprised of a variety of skill and competition levels.

Of course, you want to compete in tournaments that test your abilities and take you to the next level, but aren't completely out of your reach. For instance, if you have clearly moved forward out of local tournaments and are excelling at the intra/inter-state level, playing back in a local level tournament just to boast a win sends the wrong message. By the same token, jumping from local area tournaments into national tournaments, competing against competition above your skill level also sends the wrong message to a coach. Finding competitive national tournaments, which stretch you to compete at a higher level while still maintaining a good showing of your capabilities is a challenging task. Assess yourself honestly; know the fields at different tournaments and learn what is best for you, personally, to be competitive and to grow incrementally. This will give you the best results and put you in the right position when planning your tournament schedules.

One of the most widely recognized national tour organizations is the American Junior Golf Association (AJGA). The AJGA offers national tournaments across the nation and are very professionally run, raising your level of play significantly.

Most AJGA tournaments are three day tournaments with a cut on day two. This means you must score a specific two day combined score or lower (based on the field of junior golfers at the tournament) in order to advance to day three. The AJGA is one of the most competitive junior golf tours and well worth enlisting in.

The AJGA works on a "star and exemption" performance system, which is described on their website. If you don't have enough exemptions to be chosen for a particular tournament, you are able to earn a spot through qualifiers, which the AJGA offers prior to most tournaments. As we've mentioned, you also have the ability to earn exemptions through play in other tournaments; pay close attention to which tournaments offer AJGA exemptions. The AJGA offers yearly presentations on how their tournaments, exemption system, and qualifications work. You'll want to thoroughly research their website at www.ajga.org, call them with questions, and attend their seminars, if you can.

The AJGA also sponsors a series of invitational events for select top players, where you can be assured to see a large gathering of college coaches. The tournaments listed below are by invitation-only, and there are a variety of ways to earn an invitation. Check the AJGA website for their invitational criteria for each individual tournament.

Rolex Girls Junior Championship	**FootJoy Invitational**
Rolex Tournament of Champions	**The PING Invitational**
The Junior PLAYER Championship	**Canon Cup**
Polo Junior Golf Classic	

There are a few other national tours definitely worth mentioning. They also hold several national events and are very professionally run, with the soon to be college golfer in mind. The PGA Junior Series holds a 10-12 event series from coast to coast during the summer months, which are nationally ranked, and junior golfers have the ability to earn their way into **The Junior PGA Championship** and/or **The Callaway Golf Junior World Championship.** Check their website at www.pgajuniorseries.com for more information on how their tour is run, and which players qualify for the Championship exemptions.

The Future Collegians World Tour (FCWT) is designed with junior golfers who have not graduated from high school (up to 19 years old) in mind. They offer a year round country wide series, culminating in overall Championship tournaments at some of the best golf courses in the country. This tour is specifically designed to take the junior high school golfer to the next level of competition. Their tournaments are extremely well run and competitive. Check their website at www.fcwtgolf.com for further information.

The International Junior Golf Tour (IJGT) is a long standing, and well known organization, which offers a year round series of tournaments for junior golfers under 19, across the U.S. and in Mexico, Canada, and Scotland. The IJGT is very well established and runs professional grade tournaments on challenging courses. Many of their nationally ranked tournaments offer exemptions into other major junior tours and championships. Check their website at www.ijgt.com for further information.

A notable organization that has really taken off in the past few years is the College Golf Combines. This group holds summer tournaments and skill level assessments across the U.S., specifically designed to bring college coaches and prospective student-athletes together in a competitive golf setting. Check their website at www.collegegolfcombines.com for further information.

Some national junior championships, which every junior golfer should consider, are listed below. These are just a few of the more prestigious national championships which attract college coaches and top notch players. Check their websites for more information.

U.S. Girls Junior Championship	**Women's Western Junior**
Western Junior Championship	**Junior PGA Championship**
Junior World Golf Championship	**Southern Jr. Championship**
U.S. Junior Amateur Championship	

Typically, each of the above tournaments offers qualifier rounds either through another tour group or individually. When researching these tournaments, you will find various qualifying sites in your area with dates, deadlines, etc. The qualifiers vary in format, length, and players taken. Carefully read the eligibility and rules sections for these qualifiers and tournaments; they may be different from the tournaments you play normally .

As you advance in your tournament development, you may want to consider testing the waters and see how you stack up against college students and/or national adult players. We've heard from several coaches that they like to see junior golfers stretch themselves, and try the qualifying rounds for some of the national USGA tournaments. You can find detailed information for these tournaments on the USGA website (www.usga.org). The qualifying rounds themselves can be very intense and you get a feel for collegiate golf and beyond. Remember to maintain your amateur status when playing in these rounds, and pay very close attention to the amateur rules at the USGA and NCAA Eligibility Center. It is vitally important to sustain your amateur status to compete in college sports. Check the rules before you play. Some of the more common qualifiers at this level are:

U.S. Women's Open	U.S. Open
U.S. Women's Amateur Public Links	U.S. Amateur Public Links
U.S. Women's Amateur	U.S. Amateur

Please visit our website at www.acollegegolfplan.com for an extensive list of junior golf tour websites and links.

Chapter 3

Choosing the Right College(s) for You

There are so many aspects to choosing the right college for your individual needs, and adding a sport sometimes narrows your choices, but can also complicate your search. So, where does one begin? We've provided you with considerable fundamental information and a list of questions to ask yourself, which will get you on the right track. Additionally, staying organized throughout this process, and later in college, is crucial to your success. Our section on time management goes into great detail on how to stay focused and organized, from your high school research and marketing right through to your college years.

Be honest with yourself when answering the questions provided, and stay open minded. You might be surprised at your answers. We have found that starting with a broad group and narrowing down to a handful is the best strategy, instead of beginning with a narrow group and working your way to a broad group. This may seem obvious, however we have been in plenty of situations where it was suggested that we (and others) begin with a very narrow handful of schools based on limiting constraints. As it turns out, this is the wrong approach. While evaluating your limitations, academically, athletically, regionally, and financially is important, completely understanding how far you can reach within your constraints is a very crucial concept not often conveyed properly. We will discuss this concept in further detail in our section on **"Assessing Yourself."**

After reviewing the information in this chapter and answering the questions, use your resources to gather a list of prospects. The best place to begin your search is www.collegeboard.com. At collegeboard.com, you are able to run searches based on college size, region, state, sports, majors, GPA, testing scores and more. It is a valuable resource of college information, which includes an incredible amount of information.

Assessing Yourself

Assessing yourself can be a challenging endeavor, more mentally than physically. However, it is an absolutely necessary step in the process. First, truly assessing all of your abilities (academically and athletically) gives you an excellent idea of where you stand amongst the seemingly endless amount of colleges. By taking this one step, you begin with a comprehensive list of viable schools.

Second, college coaches know when you don't take the step to assess yourself against their school. They receive hundreds, if not thousands, of letters, resumes, and videos and, all too often, a large percentage of them are not qualified, in one way or another, to attend their school or be on their golf team. Showing them you've done your homework and sending your information to schools you are qualified for, indicates that you have taken a mature, educated approach to your college search. Coaches often mention how appreciative they are of a junior golfer who takes time to properly research schools; it significantly reduces their work and clutter.

That being said, reaching a bit above your academics, athletics, location requirements, and/or finances is an excellent starting point. You never know where you'll end up and what is out there for you, if you don't begin with a broad vision.

Assessing yourself is an area where many students and their parents don't want to face the reality of where they actually stand both academically and athletically. On the academic side however, you may be pleasantly surprised. Most college academic requirements offer a fairly wide range of acceptance levels, and you will likely find that you are in the median or upper range at a good variety of schools.

All too often, though, parents and junior golfers assume they are a top candidate for a highly ranked Division I golf school, when, in essence, they are not. Unless you have played in events such as the Junior Amateur and/or Junior World, it is tough to appreciate the wealth of talented junior golfers nationally and internationally, and where you really fit into the overall standings. Be realistic in assessing where you stand on the scale of Divisions. Many times we hear from parents and junior golfers that they wasted a lot of time thinking they were slated for a top 50 Division I school, when, in actuality, they were better suited for a lesser ranked Division I school, or one of the other Divisions or Organizations. But, their realization came too late. By the time they recognized that a different Division or Organization was a better fit for them, most of the spots were already filled. Don't let this be you. Assessing yourself openly and honestly is a critical first step to beginning your college search and eventually marketing yourself effectively.

Sit down with those who know you best and, more importantly, with a neutral third party who doesn't know you personally, and really evaluate every aspect of your game and your academics. These two components go hand in hand when attempting to be recruited. Remember, student precedes athlete in the phrase, student-athlete, for a reason. Without strong academics, it is difficult for a coach to offer you a spot without seriously petitioning on your behalf with admissions. With so many talented junior golfers, and a limited number of college team spots, this may be too much to ask of a coach, especially if your golf ability is border line for his/her university.

Establish your GPA where you stand at this moment. Your high school counselor can pull your grades and give you an updated GPA number. If you have taken the SAT and ACT, also pull those numbers (you can find your SAT number at www.collegeboard.com and your ACT number at www.actstudent.org). If you have not taken the SAT or ACT, but have taken the PSAT, use your PSAT number. The PSAT is a reasonable indicator of where your scores

ASSESSING YOURSELF

may fall on the SAT. The PSAT numbers for Critical Reading and Math are each numbers out of 80, whereas the SAT Critical Reading and Math are numbers out of 800 (most schools do not use the SAT writing number as an acceptance indicator). Therefore, when evaluating your PSAT scores against possible SAT scores, simply add a "0" to the PSAT scores to give you an idea of where you may score when taking the SAT.

Now that you are armed with all the academic numbers colleges use to determine acceptance, move forward in researching colleges that fit you academically. Research colleges' average acceptance GPA, SAT, and ACT scores (you can do this by researching the college's website and/or using collegeboard.com). It's wise to reach a little on these standards; having your academics fall in the mid to upper range is where you want to begin your initial assessment. If a school's academics are just a bit above yours, don't rule them out yet. Again, be honest, don't hope for your GPA to go up, or assume your next standardized test will be better. Look at where you are academically, at this moment, and base your comparison on your existing numbers. This evaluation will give you a strong sense of where you fall academically across a good selection of schools, and will generate a broad list.

Having a neutral third party assist in your golf evaluation is extremely helpful. They will simply look at your scores/finishes the same way a coach will, without personal and emotional bias. This may be a bit hard to swallow for some junior golfers and their parents; however, it is absolutely necessary to get a true picture of your golf ability compared to a college team.

When determining where you fit in athletically, examine *all* of your tournament finishes over the past couple of years. Really look at your scores and your finishes. When formulating your overall scoring average, don't fudge your numbers thinking, "if only I hadn't tripled on that hole, I really would have had"....or, "it was so windy that day, I really would have had"....or, "if John hadn't been in the field, I really would have won," etc. ***Do not make excuses***, be truthful and frank with yourself, and come up with an accurate number. Use all of your scores to establish an average – even that

86 you shot last summer. Coaches will be investigating all of your tournament finishes, and so should you.

Also take note of the field and the course yardages at each tournament. If you won a tournament in a smaller field playing at 6,000 yards, your score and finish will not translate well against a nationally ranked yardage/score/finish. After gathering all of your scores and finishes, place them in categories of local tournaments, inter/intra-state tournaments, and national and international tournaments. Collegiate golf is the *next* level above and beyond national/international tournaments. When evaluating your possible standing on a college team, national/international tournaments (and some higher level intra/inter-state tournaments) will always give you, and a coach, the best example of your ability. National tournaments are a closer illustration of the level of play, course slopes, and yardages, to college tournaments.

Once you have established a quality, well informed idea of your collegiate level ability, compare your scores to the overall yearly average of the colleges on your list (research the school's website and/or use the Golfweek rankings to find college averages). This comparison provides a good estimate as to where you may stand against a college team's average.

Additionally, evaluate your scores against each of the finishes of that college's top five (the traveling players) roster over the past year. This evaluation gives you a good determination of where you may fit, individually, in that particular team environment. If it is your intention to play serious, dedicated collegiate travel team golf, with room for growth and improvement, then estimating your scoring average in the mid range of a college team's top five players is an excellent fit for you.

Generally speaking the top half (ranked from about 1-150) of Division I men's teams are looking for junior golfers who have a scoring average *below* 75. Schools ranked in the bottom half (150-300+) of Division I, and the majority of Division II, are looking for a scoring average of 74.5 to 85. Division III schools are different in their requirements and aren't able to give athletic scholarships,

ASSESSING YOURSELF

however, largely, they are also looking for players with scoring averages from 75 to 88 or better.

For women, it's a bit different. While women's golf has become increasingly more competitive, it is still very probable for a junior female golfer to receive interest from Division I schools with a scoring average in the 80s.

Of course, these are not rigid rules, but should give you a general idea of where you stand based on your national level scoring average.

College coaches are typically looking to recruit players who can play in a team's top three spots. Coaches know full well that you may end up in their fourth, fifth, or lower spots, but they are not regularly looking to recruit, and give scholarships to, players who will not be an immediate significant asset to the team.

We can't express enough to be realistic and honest while assessing your ability. The worst thing is to miss a golden opportunity at a better suited institution because you inflated your skill ability. If you are significantly on the higher or lower end of a college team's average score(s), then this is, more than likely, not the team for you.

Deciding exactly what you are looking for in a team, what level of effort you want to put into collegiate golf, and how much golf will play in your college and future life, are vital elements to consider during your assessment. If you are looking for a team where you can be a successful, extremely dedicated, contributing member with room for advancement, then focus on the mid to upper levels of that college's golf team. With this level of dedication, you won't want to focus on easily being the number one player all of the time, or the lowest ranked player, offering you little hope of valuable playing time.

However, if you desire to play in every tournament without a great deal of work, then definitely look at school's where your scoring average is above their top player's average. Or, if you wish to play collegiate golf for the camaraderie and general athleticism, but are not necessarily interested in consistent travel tournament play, or major advancement, then scoring at the lower end of their field is your best fit. Bear in mind, though, that joining a collegiate team on the lower end with little desire to advance will, more than likely, not result in much of, if any, golf scholarship money. If this is where your thinking is, you may want to look at a lesser ranked school, a different Division, Organization, Intramural, or Club golf team.

Get a feeling for where you want to be in the overall scheme of a team's roster, and how much effort you want to put into collegiate golf. After all of your research and evaluation, it is critical to be honest with yourself and, especially, with your parents. Knowing where you want to fit in on a team, is a key component. This should be the best fit for **you**, not someone else's idea of where you **should** fit in. Put a lot of time and thought into your ideal team environment and communicate that with your family members.

If you are interested in pursuing a golf scholarship, then focus on schools just above, right at, and all of those below your self-assessed golf skill level. Do the same when assessing your GPA/SAT/ACT scores. This grouping will generate the most interest, both academically and athletically. This is the best place to begin your college list and narrow it down as you investigate other requirements.

Other areas to take into consideration are location, school size, college majors, class size, faith, finances and more. Unless you are 150% sure that you want the best Marine Biology school in the country, staying very open minded on these requirements is highly recommended. All too often, students and parents place too much emphasis on these types of constraints during their *initial* assessment, and rule out many opportunities. Backtracking, after realizing you were too limited during your search, rarely turns out well for the student-athlete. Stay extremely open minded and understand that most schools offer an abundance of excellent educational choices, financial aid opportunities, academic and athletic scholarships, etc.

ASSESSING YOURSELF

At this point, you should have a well informed list. Take some time to organize your list on the computer; a spreadsheet program works best, giving you the ability to sort your list in any fashion. Having your list laid out in front of you, in one place, gives you a good sense of where you are going from here. It allows you to stay focused, keep good notes, really evaluate each school, save time, and determine your next steps.

The following are some suggestions on headers to include on your list:

COLLEGE LIST SPREADSHEET HEADER SUGGESTIONS

Institution Name	Total Undergrad Enrollment
Coach's First Name	GPA Median Requirements
Coach's Last Name	SAT Median Requirements
Coach's Phone	ACT Median Requirements
Coach's Email	Date(s) Correspondence Sent
College Mailing Address	Date(s) Response(s) Received
College City, State, Zip (3 Columns)	In-State / Out of State Tuition
College Type (Public/Private)	Notes

Researching Colleges

Once you have a qualified list of schools, study each college's website to further examine all of your requirements. Look at admission requirements, pictures, virtual tours, majors, athletic programs, student life and more. Review their overall athletic program to see if they offer a good variety of sports, and what their level of administrative support is from the Athletic Director on down. Check into their golf team stats, roster, and schedule and read the bios provided on their website. Examine their golf team roster for the amount of juniors and seniors currently on their team to assess the number of future players they may need. Really take your time working your way through their website, and request brochures and information. The more informed you are, the better opportunities you have.

To further your research utilize Golfweek's rankings for Division I schools, if you are interested in Division I schools and feel you fit into this environment both academically and athletically. These rankings change constantly as team's play in their season tournaments. However, it is a good general indication of where the different schools rank, and their overall team averages.

There are many excellent colleges in all of the Divisions and Organizations, which can afford you a phenomenal education and a great athletic experience. As you narrow your search, stay within the boundaries you have established for yourself, based on **your** personal assessment. Do not "reach" yourself out of contention with a school that is better suited to your abilities. By the same token, do not rule a school out because it may not have the big name, or be ranked where **you** think it ought to be.

Questions to Ask Yourself

Remember, your intention is to play golf in college, so this limits some of the normal questions other students may ask themselves, such as "what intramural sports do they have" or "do they have semester travel abroad programs."

We recommend taking a pen and paper and answering each question in the most honest way possible. However, we can't say enough to stay open minded, as things often turn out a lot differently than you think. For instance, you may think you want a large school with a very serious high level golf team, but after many visits, you may realize that a smaller environment is just the thing for you.

Be honest with yourself about your future goals – do you intend to try and be a touring professional or are you just looking for the camaraderie, discipline, and experience of playing college golf? Would you like a career in the golf world that doesn't include a tour professional? Is education or golf most important to you when attending college? Remember, it is a very small percentage (a fraction of 1 percent) of college golfers who end up as touring professionals. Earning a degree and becoming a productive citizen, in or out of the golf world, is the most important part of your educational experience.

As far as our personal experience goes, we started looking at only in-state public schools. We quickly realized that with good golf scholarships, academic scholarships, and aid, out-of-state and private schools actually are just as cost effective, and often offer a superior education and environment. This realization opened many doors we never knew were there before.

After many visits, and listening to our teen say, "this isn't what I expected college to look like," we realized he had a vision that he couldn't describe. At one particular visit, he finally said, "Now this is a college." We took a long look around at the buildings, the professors, the rooms, even the amount of grass and trees, and understood what he was looking for – now we knew where to focus our search. We were **very** far from where we had started, so keeping an open mind is absolutely essential.

Questions:

- What is my main reason for going to college? Am I looking to play college golf while getting an education or am I looking to get an education while playing college golf?

- What size school population do I feel is right for me?
  - Under 2,000
  - 2,000 – 5,000
  - 5,000 – 15,000
  - 15,000 – 25,000
  - 25,000+

- What are my GPA, SAT, and ACT scores?

- Where do I fit in with these numbers?

- What do I want to major in – does this school offer that major?

- How far away from home am I willing to go?

- What state, area, region, would I like to look at? Am I willing to broaden my location requirements?

- What kind of schools can I afford – public in-state only, and/or public out-of-state, and/or private?

- Do I qualify for financial aid or an academic scholarship?

- What is my likelihood of getting a golf scholarship?

- What is important to me at a school – a good library, a good recreation center, good dorm rooms, a variety of food choices, etc.?

- Is a faith-based college important to me?

- What kind of town environment am I looking for surrounding the college? Do I want a lot of shops/restaurants around, a big city, a medium size town or am I okay with an out of the way college?

- Where do I fit on a golf team based on my overall tournament average?

- Do I want something a bit above or below where I feel I fit in?

- Do I want to pursue only NCAA Division I or am I open to Division II, III, NAIA, or NJCAA?

- How important is a golf scholarship to me – am I willing or able to play without a scholarship?

- How many students are currently on a particular college's team and how many are seniors?

- How many spots may be open on a particular college's team?

- Do I want a school where I am guaranteed to play in tournaments my freshman year, or am I okay with "sitting the bench" my freshman year and working my way into the program?

- Is a start up golf program a good fit for me or do I want a long running, well established program?

- Do I want an area where I can practice golf year round, or do I want an area that affords me some time off?

QUESTIONS TO ASK YOURSELF

- What kind of overall athletic program am I looking for – larger program with a huge variety of sports or a smaller program which may only have a few sports?

- What kind of practice facilities am I looking for? Do I want a school that has at least one on-site course or am I okay with off-site local courses? Do I want a school that has an indoor practice facility?

- Is it important to me to have a full time coaching staff or am I okay with a part time coaching staff?

- Do I want an extremely serious, highly dedicated golf program or am I looking for something a little more laid back?

- Do I feel I am on par both academically and athletically based on this school's statistics?

- Do I feel I can compete and succeed in this environment?

The College Golf Schedule

A college's golf schedule is governed by their player organization, i.e. the NCAA, NAIA, NJCAA, etc. They are permitted a certain number of practice hours in season and out of season, a certain number of tournament days per year, etc. College coaches are required to stay abreast of this information. Check with the college coaches you speak to regarding their particular schedule and their official time allotments. A typical college golf team and golf schedule will look something like the following. Most college golf teams range from 7-17 players, with the average being about 9-10, and five usually travel and play in tournaments. Coaches use a variety of systems to identify their travel players, often holding qualifiers per tournament and/or per season. This is usually fairly similar to the way high school coaches coordinate their team travel systems, so you may be familiar with a college coach's system.

A college golf team's fall season typically runs from the beginning of a college fall semester to the end of October, and they play about five to six tournaments, during this season. November through January or February is their "off season." Their spring season begins in February or March and, again, they play about five to six tournaments. If we've heard it once, we've heard it from twenty or more coaches, that the golf team is typically the most traveled team on campus because a large amount of their tournaments tend to fall on Monday's and Tuesday's.

A typical in season college day is extremely full. Again, college athletics are limited to the number of hours they can schedule workouts and practices by their governing organization; check with the coach regarding his/her particular schedule and time/day allotments. Most teams have early morning workouts and afternoon practices, with their college academic curriculum scheduled in between. You may have a 6 or 7 a.m. workout, classes from 8 a.m. to 3 p.m., and golf practice from 3:30 to 5:30 p.m. Combine this with, possibly, twenty days of missed classes for travel, and it is quite a demanding schedule. A college golf team member's schedule may look something like the schedule on the next page.

THE COLLEGE GOLF SCHEDULE

	Mon	Tue	Wed	Thur	Fri	Sat	Sun
SAMPLE COLLEGE GOLF SCHEDULE							
7-8 am	Workout with Trainer		Workout with Trainer		Workout with Trainer		
8-12 pm	Eat / Classes / Study	Eat / Classes / Study	Eat / Classes / Study	Eat / Classes / Study	Eat / Classes / Study	Breakfast Rec Time	Brunch Rec Time
1-3 pm	Classes / Study	Classes / Study	Classes / Study	Classes / Study	Classes / Study	Study	Golf Practice
3:30-5:30 pm	Labs Study	Golf Practice	Labs / Golf Practice	Golf Practice	Golf Practice	Golf Practice	Golf Practice
6-8 pm	Dinner Rest Study	Dinner Rest Study	Dinner Rest Study	Dinner Rest Study	Dinner Rest Study	Dinner Rest Study	Dinner Rest Study
8-11 pm	Study	Study	Study	Study			Study

Does Not Include Tournament Travel Time

This schedule allows little time to get all of your college work done and squeeze in a bit of social time. Collegiate golf team members have to become masters of time management, and utilize every resource offered to them on campus. College athletes are offered on campus free tutoring and, typically, the athletic department also offers scheduled study groups. Many schools have athletic counselors available to help you stay on track with your class schedule and load. Staying abreast of the resources available to you, and utilizing them fully, is very key to a successful academic-athletic collegiate relationship.

Time Management – Now and Later

Organizing your time and staying abreast of what needs to be done and when you need to do it, is paramount to your success now and, later, as a collegiate student-athlete. When choosing colleges to add to your list, having an organized system in place to stay up to date on all of your assessments and guidelines is essential.

Additionally, successfully completing your high school years with excellent grades, a distinguished golf career both on the high school team and, especially, in national junior tournaments, marketing yourself to college coaches, visiting colleges, applying to colleges, undertaking some volunteer work and, possibly, holding down a part time job are monumental tasks and require a very focused time management system. Likewise, as you enter your college years as a student-athlete, similar demands require the same diligent focus and level of organization.

Without a time management system in place, it becomes difficult to competently complete all of your tasks and stay on track, without something falling through the cracks. By following a few simple guidelines and suggestions, you can successfully navigate your way through high school, college, golf, and work efficiently and effectively. Beginning now and staying focused and disciplined, will carry you through all the different stages of your life. Additionally, organizing all of the different elements on your plate, reduces your stress and provides you with more time to relax and enjoy yourself.

Get a calendar that works for you:

With the advent of computers and the availability of having your calendar, contacts, phone numbers, addresses, email and more on a personal mobile device, it is difficult to suggest anything other than a computer software calendar. Most, if not all, computers and smart phones come preloaded with a calendar that is completely integrated with your contact list, your email, your texts, etc., and also provides you with the ability to synch your computer to phone and vice versa. Your biggest issue is choosing the computer, phone (or PDA), and software that works best for you – the right combination is definitely out there amongst the enormous plethora of devices available.

However, if today's technology simply does not fit your needs, a good day planner is the other option. There are many excellent day planners', organized in different ways, to suit everyone's personal needs. You can find a good variety at office supply stores and online.

Input EVERYTHING into your calendar:

Yes, we mean everything, or just about everything, anyway (we certainly aren't suggesting inputting restroom breaks). We realize that everyone needs some flexibility, spontaneity, fun and quiet time, and scheduling those times would defeat their purpose. However, scheduling all of your other necessary tasks makes the "fun" times more attainable and enjoyable. Having your tasks clearly slotted and laid out in front of you affords you the peace of mind of knowing what needs to be done, doing it in a timely manner, and having time for recreation and relaxation.

Keeping a calendar similar to the "Sample Golf Schedule" we presented a few pages ago, is a good place to start. First, input your daily items, such as:

* Your academic course times
* Your scheduled golf practices
* Your scheduled workout times

- Your work hours (if you work, do volunteer work, or are on a work study program in college)
- Meal times

Secondly, input your weekly and monthly items, such as:

- Your work hours, if they are weekly (if you work, do volunteer work, or are on a work study program in college)
- Your golf tournaments, and travel
- Class assignments (most teachers and professors give a syllabus which outlines class assignments and major projects, with their due dates)
- Any other weekly or monthly items that require a good amount of time, such as laundry, etc.
- Also input any "special" items you may have coming up such as a vacation, a trip home (if you are in college), a visitor(s) coming to see you, doctor's appointments, counselor appointments, teacher reviews, etc.

Schedule study time:

First input all of your scheduled study groups or tutoring time, if any. Typically, college athletes are offered scheduled study group sessions and free tutoring time. Your coach will often have study group time scheduled for you and your teammates. Schedule this time on your calendar first.

Utilizing free tutoring sessions is an extremely efficient use of your time, and most college student-athletes do not use this service enough. One coach mentioned that scheduling weekly tutoring time for each course is one of the best ways to schedule your course study time. Scheduling weekly time with a tutor makes you accountable to a time slot with another person and, in essence, forces you to "show up" and get your work done. In addition, sitting with a tutor can do nothing but help you with your coursework and, more than likely, saves you a lot of "struggle" time in the long run.

Additionally, while still in high school, most teachers offer tutor time in the mornings and/or afternoons – again, using this time will

TIME MANAGEMENT – NOW & LATER

help with your workload and is time efficient. Utilize the resources given to you!

Carefully review all of your scheduled study group time and tutor time, if any. Then, review your course workload. It is recommended that for every credit hour of course time, a college student should prepare for approximately two hours of study time. A college student carrying a 15 hour credit load would then require 30 hours of study time per week; that means a total of 45 hours of academics per week! For the high school student, this number is reduced by about half, depending on your course load. However, for the junior golfer determined to be a college golfer, this "free" time is filled with research, creating resumes, cover letters and swing videos, marketing, following up with college coaches, visiting college campuses and coaches, etc.

Of course, each course requires a different study workload at different times. For instance, some courses only require weekly reading assignments with major projects and/or papers at the end of the month or semester; while others require more extensive assignments each day/week with either mini projects interspersed, or none at all. Evaluate your courses and thoroughly review your syllabuses to estimate your study time for each course effectively.

Make a list of all of your major projects/papers and their due dates. Input those items into your calendar. Estimate how much time you will need for each project/paper – overestimating is key here. Most students tend to underestimate the time needed for major projects/papers and end up frazzled, pulling all nighters just before they are due. Don't let this be you, double the time you think it will take, and you should be right on track. Just think, if you've overestimated and finish "early," that's more relaxation time you hadn't planned on, and a very nice surprise.

Knowing when a project/paper is due gives you the opportunity to schedule time intervals each week to work on it little by little. Scheduling small bits of time for major projects/papers is so important to successfully managing your coursework. We know most students tend to procrastinate, but avoiding this temptation will *really* serve you well in the long run. Everything around you will run more smoothly, especially your golf, when you are not panicked about a project or paper you have put off, which is due the next day. This is especially true for a sport like golf, which is so much more of a mental game than any other collegiate sport. You really need to have your "head in the game" to be successful, so keeping the other components of your life organized and on track is absolutely crucial.

After a thorough review of your workload, pre-scheduled study groups, and tutor time, **input specific coursework assignments into your study groups and tutor time.** If a college student has two 2-hour study group sessions scheduled per week, and schedules 1 ½ to 2 hours of tutor time per week, per course, then already approximately 15 hours of study time is pre-scheduled, without even really working at it!

Now, look at the open slots on your calendar and input another 10-15 hours of study time for college students. This will not be as difficult as it sounds, there will still be plenty of open slots on your calendar, if you have worked with it properly. It is recommended that students try to schedule study time at approximately the same time each day, when possible. This creates good learning and study habits.

For high school junior golfers, schedule your college research and marketing time into those same 10 hours per week of available time on your calendar. This may sound like a lot of time, but you will be surprised how much time it takes to research and market yourself proficiently. Again, forcing yourself to sit down each day around the same time to research, update your information, follow up, communicate with coaches, schedule visits, etc. will become an important habit which will translate well into your college years.

Schedule study/work breaks:

Studies have shown that taking a 15-minute break for every one to one and a half hours of work/study time is beneficial, and proves much more effective than if you hadn't taken a break. The body needs a break from sitting in front of a computer, reading, working, or doing math or science problems. A few minute break actually helps keep you more focused and on task. Physically scheduling this time on your calendar reminds you of how important a break is and helps you plan your time.

A break means grabbing a snack or drink, walking around, stretching, etc. It doesn't mean getting deeply involved in a t.v. show or movie, or chatting for hours with friends. Stay focused on your scheduled study time.

Learn to multitask and use time efficiently:
Some of my best study times, during college, were spent in the laundry room. A load of laundry takes approximately one hour to wash and one hour to dry. The end of each load reminds you to take your break, and affords you the opportunity to walk around and stretch while moving your laundry from washer to dryer. And, to top it all off, you are multi-tasking, completing two necessary tasks at the same time! This is a great example of using your time wisely.

If you have two classes with 30-40 minutes in between, instead of using that time to go back to the dorm or chat it up, find a quiet spot to study. Using these small time slots efficiently saves time later for other interests or golf practice time.

Review your calendar to identify those small time slots in your calendar to use for "quick" study moments when you need to read a chapter or finish a few math problems, etc.

Save time for rest and relaxation:
At this point, your calendar will be pretty full. However, if you planned well, you should have plenty of slots (preferably during weekend nights) for social time and relaxation. Staying on task and paying attention to your calendar will definitely allow you stress free relaxation time.

Additionally, we all need time to rest and sleep. Physically scheduling those times on your calendar prompts you to take the proper amount of time to physically recharge. Everyone is different when it comes to the amount of time they need to sleep and rest. By now, you should have a good idea of how your body works best, and the amount of time you need during different times of the day to recharge. Input these times on your calendar.

Keep an updated "to do" list:

Staying on target with your assignments is absolutely critical to your time management. Keeping an on-going, updated to do list is essential. Remove and update items on your list as they are completed, or parts of them are accomplished. This is such an easy thing to do with today's software management programs. Again, utilize your resources.

For the high school golfer, also use your spreadsheet, which we discussed earlier in this chapter, to stay on task with your college golf recruiting. Stay on top of your updates, and keep yourself apprised of where you stand with each school. Update your notes section after each correspondence with a coach, remove schools that you feel are no longer viable options, highlight schools which are very interested, etc. Transfer "to do" information from your spreadsheet into your to do list and calendar to stay current.

Use your "to do" list for everything including items you need to buy and/or return, people you need to call, appointments you need to schedule, golf shots you need to work on, etc., in addition to your academic assignments. Keeping all of these items constantly updated in one place, saves time when running to the store, scheduling appointments, making calls, etc.

Notify your teachers/professors of scheduled absences:

As we mentioned earlier, high school and college golfers spend a great deal of time traveling for tournaments. Knowing your upcoming travel tournament schedule and discussing your future absences with your teachers/professors allows time to plan. Taking your travel tournament schedule to your teachers gives, both, you, and them an opportunity to review your dates and plan for the assignments you will miss.

TIME MANAGEMENT – NOW & LATER

Be mature and respectful when approaching your professor with these absences. Professors are there to impart wisdom and education and not to cater to arrogant athletes. Any extra help or time they give you is a gift, and should be treated as such. If a professor is not willing to work with your travel tournament schedule, then work on your own, or with your coach, to balance your travel time and assignments efficiently.

Print your calendar out:

Each week, print your calendar out with side bar "to do" items, upcoming appointments, travel, college recruiting tasks, and projects. Place your calendar where you'll see it every day, on your bulletin board, on your mirror, stuck to a notebook, etc. Physically seeing your schedule each day will save you time, promote staying on task, remind you of upcoming events, etc. Reviewing your calendar each day is a very important and necessary to step to time management.

Keep your calendar workload in front of you at all times. You will reap the benefits of successfully navigating your way through these complex times by staying focused and organized. As we said earlier, it all seems to fall into place, almost effortlessly, with a well-organized time management schedule.

Chapter 4

Marketing Yourself

Learning to market yourself, and putting your name and accomplishments into the hands of a college golf coach, is one of the most important aspects of this process. College coaches are extremely busy and, unless you are ranked amongst the top 50-100 junior golfers in the nation, they don't have time to research you and come knocking on your door. You have to "knock on their door."

Do not wait for someone to do the work for you – this is your game and you, alone, are responsible for capturing college golf coaches' attention and interest. Never assume your high school coach, a counselor, or a college coach will take the lead; if you do, it may be too late.

It's a daunting process and tough to know how to begin, what to send, how to send it, and when to send what. This chapter will work you through a solid course of action to deliver your credentials into a coach's file. Marketing yourself may be an area where you want to seek consulting assistance, if you find it too time consuming and/or overwhelming. Be leery, though, of recruiters who offer you the whole package for an exorbitant price and ridiculous guarantees. If you choose to utilize a recruiter or consultant, ask a lot of questions to determine precisely what services they will actually be providing. So many times we have seen recruiters offer services, which they never actually fulfill; they end up only directing you to do all of the work.

Arm yourself with information, and acquire a written agreement stating what work will be completed by both parties (you and the consultant/recruiter). More than likely, you'll want to delegate the pieces you require assistance with, and do the rest yourself. This approach will alleviate much of your burden, and allow you time to focus on the many other factors involved in this process.

The foremost thing to remember is that you are selling a package, not just a golfer. College coaches don't have time to overwork in their effort to acquire a specific golfer with problematic issues, when there is an abundance of talent available. It is paramount to keep your grades up, do well on your standardized tests, conduct yourself in a respectful manner at all times, be honest, show integrity, dress appropriately, project a clean and well groomed image, contain your extreme emotions on and off the course, consistently prove your quest to better yourself and your game, and, of course, play golf to the absolute best of your ability.

This may seem like an awesome task for a teenager, but compiling it all into a nice, clean, crisp package, may very well give you the leverage you need. After all, it is your dream to play collegiate golf, therefore, it is your responsibility to be disciplined and organized enough to succeed.

We have assembled guidelines to help you build that package, and advertise yourself at the right time to the right people.

All About Resumes, Letters and Swing Videos

Your cover letter, resume, and swing video are the most important elements to marketing yourself. These three items are the first impression a coach receives, representing who you are and your abilities. They should be well organized, informative, and concise.

We have provided examples of resumes and letters at the end of this chapter, however, keep in the back of your mind, that this is another area where you may consider hiring consulting assistance. Furthermore, we highly encourage you to explore professionals to create an expertly crafted swing video.

The Cover Letter:

The cover letter is your first introduction to a college coach. Furnish the coach with a concise, informational look at who you are academically and athletically. Keep your cover letter to one page maximum, and **ALWAYS** personalize it towards that specific coach and his/her university. College golf coaches have commented that they prefer personal letters; they have no interest in generic letters and definitely oppose letters from recruiters.

Your heading is determined by your chosen method of sending your letter. If you are mailing it via postal mail, then you will want to include a postal standard header with:

* Date
* Attn: Coach's Name
* XYZ University
* Coach's specific mail box at the University
* Street Address
* City, State Zip Code

If you are sending your letters via email, use the header as an opportunity to advertise your information such as prominently displaying your name, address, email information, and phone number at the top of your email. You have more leeway in an email to be creative in your heading. See our different heading examples at the end of this chapter.

ALWAYS begin with Dear Coach [Coach's Last Name]. This first line immediately exhibits personalization and draws the coach's attention further into your letter and resume.

There are varying approaches to arranging your letter, but overall you'll want to acquaint the coach with your name, your grade, your high school name, its UIL ranking (i.e. 5A, 4A, etc.), and your town, in the first paragraph. Information on your GPA and academic accolades should be prominently discussed. Highlight recent exceptional golf tournaments, both high school and national. Coaches are pursuing versatile, athletic students. Mentioning a job, volunteer work, other athletics, and interests, should be conveyed.

Point them in the direction of your resume by stating it is attached (or below), and focuses on your academic achievements, golf tournament finishes, and upcoming tournament schedule.

It is important to place some emphasis on how you, personally, will fit into their university, both academically and athletically. This demonstrates you've taken time to research their school and their team.

If this particular university is definitely one of your top choices, communicate your desire in your cover letter – coaches want to know where they stand in your line up, as much as you want to know where you stand in theirs. Be proactive and affirm your intentions. If your athletics and academics stack up with their team and university, a coach may place you at a higher priority if made aware that their school is one of your top choices. This makes their work easier, and gives them a sense that you may actually attend their school if an offer is extended.

Always close with a thank you, a request for a response, and let them know you are looking forward to hearing from them.

Your cover letter needs to be a short, well-organized synopsis, full of information. Take your time constructing, personalizing, reviewing, and editing its contents. First impressions carry a lot of weight.

The Resume:
Your resume needs to be chock-full of information in a neat, well-organized manner, and should NEVER be more than two pages. Coaches are not looking to read a litany of every tournament you've been in since you were ten, and weeding through to locate the important highlights. A lengthy resume is a sure fire way to lose their attention fast.

The resume is a representation of who you are personally, academically, and athletically. Highlight your strongest accomplishments with only the most pertinent information.

The resume header is a quick snapshot of your personal, educational, and golf information. Include a face front photo. Avoid the temptation to use a golf swing photo; this is cliché and coaches want to see *you*, not part of you (they will see enough swings on the course and in your swing video). Your header needs to give them a quick, uncomplicated view of who you are, and entice them to keep reading.

In an organized fashion, incorporate your photo and a personal section with:

- Your name
- Full address
- Home phone number
- Your cell phone number
- Your email address
- Your birth date
- Parents' names
- Parents' home address (if different than yours)
- Parents' cell phone number (one number will suffice)
- Parents' email address (one email address will suffice)
- Some coaches prefer having your height and weight on the resume; however, we have found that most find this to be optional. It is your decision.

Integrate your High School Information in the golf resume header with:

- High School name
- High School full address
- High School coach's full name
- High School coach's contact information
- Your graduation date
- Your current grade (junior, senior, etc.)
- Your current GPA, SAT score, and ACT score (if you haven't taken your SATs or ACTs when you send out your information, simply notate that on your resume; or if you have taken them but do not have the scores yet, simply state, "taken March, 20XX," or whatever the date is that you took them).

THE RESUME

Most importantly, your header should contain brief golf information:

- Your high school stroke average (this usually includes your nine hole average and the name of the golf course where your high school team regularly practices – where your average has been established)
- Your USGA GHIN handicap and your GHIN number (giving coaches the opportunity to look up your GHIN number)
- Your overall tournament average
- Your home golf course name, if you have one
- Your home golf course address and phone number

Determining a tournament average may seem a bit difficult, but we have found it best to calculate your current tournament average from your "competition highlights," in the next section of your resume; this is a good reflection of your existing skill level.

The next section – your **competition highlights** – is central to a coach's determination of your tournament ability and level of play. We've heard varying degrees of what types of tournaments coaches want to see, ranging from many who don't place a lot of value on high school tournaments and only want to see "national" level tournament finishes, to those who place a great deal of value on high school tournaments, district, regional, and state information. Keeping this in mind, a top 25 finish in a high level national tournament weighs more heavily than a top 10 finish in an average high school tournament – however, a win is a win, and should always be prominently and proudly displayed. A solid combination of your most prominent finishes is your best representation. This area is where you shine – so, put a lot of thought and time into it.

The competition highlights section should be extremely organized and easy to read – a table format is best. Include:

- Date(s) of your tournament
- The course and town/state
- The yardage you played
- The par you played

- The rating and slope you played
- The weather conditions you played in
- The tour name
- The name of the tournament
- The type of tournament (if different from regular stroke play, such as a match play tournament, etc.)
- Your scores for each day
- Your overall score
- Your finish
- The total amount of players in the field
- Incorporate any special information, such as "made the cut," "qualified," etc.

List tournaments from newest to oldest, and include about ten to fifteen competitions (this is not a hard and fast rule, but you are portraying a good representation of your tournament ability, without overdoing it). Your most recent accomplishments are most important and you shouldn't go back too far, definitely not before your freshman year in high school. If you include freshman year achievements, they should only be those tournaments that were spectacular. This is your area to become memorable to coaches – make it shine!

The next section, your **upcoming schedule**, gives coaches the opportunity to physically watch you play, and depicts the level of your tournament capabilities. Integrate a neat table consisting of:

- The date of the tournament
- The course name
- The course city and state
- The course full physical address
- The course telephone number
- The name of the tournament
- The name of the tour

College coaches are always at national tournaments, and there is usually a board announcing which coaches are there; you never know, one of them may be there just to see you. We've actually had coaches tell us they came to a specific AJGA tournament our

THE RESUME

son was playing in because he sent them his upcoming schedule. Even if they aren't there to specifically see you, they will remember your information, once they connect your name on the board and your resume sitting in their inbox. This is an important aspect of your resume.

The **high school awards and achievements** section solidifies your overall image. Stay organized and break it out into sections, usually by high school grade. Really display your finer points in this area. Include special items such as:

* All-District
* All-Regional
* All-State
* All-Academic
* Honor Roll
* High School team finishes
* And more....

Coaches and colleges want to see how well rounded you are and what kind of other interests you have. Incorporating a section on your interests, other activities, other athletics, volunteer work, jobs, etc. demonstrates your versatility. It shows a well-rounded person with a variety of interests who is able to combine school, golf, social, and professional responsibilities.

The last part of your resume proves the existence of **references**. This is not the place to put a reference letter, but is the place to show you have references. Some suggest simply putting a typical line that states, "References Available Upon Request," which is fine. However, we advise adding a couple actual names/titles with their contact information. Adding your teaching professional and/or swing coach, with their title and contact information often proves beneficial. Don't go overboard with your references, but a couple obvious professionals you work with, will promote you in the long run.

Your resume exemplifies who you are, where you've been, what you've accomplished, and where you are going. It is indicative of your academic and athletic skill level, and your potential. Carefully choose the information you place in your resume and be attentive to details. Take time to review, edit, have others review it, rework and polish it, until it is perfect – always check spelling, grammar, and vocabulary.

The Swing Video:

When it comes to marketing yourself, nothing will bring you closer to a coach than a swing video. Having a swing video readily available, which you can immediately access and send to a college coach, is essential and shows preparedness.

Coaches receive an abundance of these videos, along with letters and resumes. Keeping their attention is both imperative and challenging. The key is to keep your video about three to five minutes long, and stick to the topic of showing them your swing. Don't be flashy and get them lost in the background. Overwhelm them with your talent, quickly and clearly. Choose a simple golf practice area without a lot of noise, other players, or general distractions.

Some swing videos have a voice-over of the golfer speaking in the background, and some do not. This is really up to you. Our opinion is, the information you would be describing is the same information that already exists in your resume. This can quickly become outdated as you progress with new tournaments. That being said, a brief introduction and a closing, from you, should always be included. This appears very professional and allows them to hear you, as well as view you.

Begin by standing in front of the camera and clearly stating your name and contact information. Such as, "My name is [your name] and I am a [your grade] at [your high school] in [town, state]. I graduate in [month, year]. Today I will be hitting [list the swings you will be showing them]. I hope you find this informative and thank you for taking the time to watch." This is a good basic introduction.

THE SWING VIDEO

As you proceed through your swings, introduce each swing type with either your voice and/or a simple caption on the screen. Use a representative sampling of clubs including wedge shots, 8-iron, 5-iron, and driver (working your way up in distance). Make sure to include two to three swings, with each club from at least two different angles, including views from the side and rear. Include your putting stroke from short and long range (lag putting).

TIP   It's *not* important to sink every putt on the swing video.

After you conclude your swings, end with you standing in front of the camera thanking them for their time. A simple, "Thank you for taking the time to watch my swing video and I look forward to your response soon," is just right. It lets them know you are appreciative and respectful of their time, and you are looking for a response in a simple, concise manner.

Creating a swing video can be a complicated matter. You need a good video camera and film editing software. If you or a family member are not extremely familiar with film editing, or you don't have the appropriate software and/or equipment, you will definitely want to seek professional assistance with this portion of your package.

While watching your swing video, coaches have the opportunity to actually *see you*, and see you in action. It is imperative that you present yourself well, be well groomed, and dressed neatly and appropriately. Take time to really look at the image you are projecting, from head to toe.

Include an introduction. Speak clearly and tell your audience who you are, and who you play for (your High School). Give a summary of the views of your game you will be highlighting, and thank your viewers, in advance, for their attention.

Optionally, include a close up on your grip.

Include swings throughout a range of clubs. Generally, starting with a wedge and working your way up through Driver. Pitching wedge, 8-iron, 5-iron and Driver, provides a great overview.

It is recommended that you provide both a side view and rear view, so coaches can evaluate your swing most effectively.

Show your putting stroke on both short putts and lag putts.

SWING VIDEO SCREEN SHOT EXAMPLES

Include views from both the front and rear.

Include a closing, thanking your viewers for their time and attention. Remember to speak clearly and communicate your aspirations for collegiate golf play.

Your Name
123 Anytown Drive
Your City, Your State 88888

Home Phone: 888.555.1212
Cell Phone: 888.555.1212

Email: youremail@gmail.com

Include a detailed closing frame with your contact information. Depending on how and where you deliver this video, make your own personal decision on how much information to expose. For social sites with a wide reach, you may want to limit personal information to an email address.

When to Send Your Information

There are no hard and fast rules on what information to send when to a coach. However, we have found that *not* sending everything at once is most effective. We highly recommend sending your cover letter and resume first as a solid introduction to who you are, and how you fit in with their team and university. Your resume also includes your upcoming schedule, giving the coach an opportunity to plan his/her tournament viewing schedule. In their response, a coach may ask to see your swing video. Obviously, immediately send any information they request.

When to send your initial communications can be confusing. We have heard everything from early in your sophomore year to summer of your junior year, from a variety of sources.

There are advantages and disadvantages to sending early. If you choose to send your package in your sophomore year, and you aren't a "highly" recruited player, it is very easy to get lost in the shuffle. However, the advantage is that your name is now on their radar – but will they remember it later on? Generally speaking, coaches are "always" recruiting, keeping their eyes and ears open for their next players. Our advice on sending early in your sophomore year is to do so only if you are a top ranked player, and/or if there is a particular school you are dead set on attending – you'll want to get your name known, if this is the case.

Typically, the highly ranked colleges are looking at players early on in that player's sophomore year of high school. If you feel this is where you fit in, begin sending your information around January to March of your sophomore year. This accommodates coaches the time to research your information, and schedule their tournament viewing to fit into your upcoming schedule. (Check the NCAA guidelines for information on when coaches can contact and/or evaluate you).

For the vast majority of junior golfers, we recommend sending your information in your junior year. Early December is an excellent time since coaches have just gone through the November signing, taken a break for Thanksgiving, and are in the off season, looking forward to their winter break. However, the disadvantage is, if they didn't get the signees they were hoping for in November, they are now reevaluating and still searching for their upcoming fall season recruits, which may leave you lost in the shuffle.

We believe that early in the second semester (January to March) of your Junior year is the best time to send your resume and cover letter (take time to check the school's calendar to verify when coaches will be back in session after the winter break – February 1 is always a safe bet). Your information reaches the coach's desk just as they are finishing their previous year's recruiting, and seriously looking at your graduation year candidates. It is the beginning of spring season when everyone is thinking about golf, and your upcoming schedule will be foremost on your mind and theirs.

Just before your summer tournaments, send coaches your swing video. The summer months are the busiest recruiting months. Sending your swing video at this point holds a two fold advantage. It gives you another opportunity to send something unique as a follow up correspondence, and it gives the coach a chance to evaluate your swing prior to physically viewing you at a tournament. Your swing video entices them to follow you at a tournament, and gives them an idea of what to expect. Additionally, if a coach does not have the chance to physically watch you play, due to distance or time constraints, your swing video gives them the opportunity to evaluate how you play. As we've said, it is the best representation of your game, barring personal viewing, and brings you closer to the coach than any other materials. Sending your swing video separately, distinguishes it from your other information and other junior golfer's materials.

Whether you hear back from a coach or not, sending regular updates (approximately every week to two weeks) with your updated schedule and/or new tournament finishes is extremely beneficial. Keeping them current on how you are progressing through the year, both academically and athletically, is indicative of your dedication to playing college golf and pursuing higher education. If there is a specific college(s) you are particularly interested in, focus your communication on them. You are building a one on one relationship with, possibly, your future golf coach; and keeping them engaged is an integral part of this process.

As we mentioned earlier, scheduling unofficial college visits around your summer tournaments is an excellent idea and use of your time. It is an indispensable part of determining your college choice, and commonly, a visit is the deciding factor as to which college you choose. See our section on **"Visiting Colleges"** for more in depth information.

After a college visit where a coach is involved, **ALWAYS** immediately send a thank you note to the coach. In your thank you note, make a concerted effort to leave the door open for further discussion and evaluation. If you feel this may be the school for you, convey your interest by enthusiastically declaring how much you can contribute and how well you feel you fit in with the team and university. Let the coach know this school is your choice, otherwise he/she may move onto others if he/she doesn't realize your level of interest. Don't be coy in these emails, if you are absolutely sure this may be the place for you.

Send your golf reference(s) once you have established a solid rapport with a coach, and particularly, after a visit. Two solid golf references are preferable – one from a teaching professional and that "special" one we described earlier, i.e. from a junior golfer's parent or someone involved in the junior golf program, etc.

Sending one reference at a time is the best approach. Forwarding your "teaching professional" reference letter first, solidifies your golf ability and resolve. Reserving the "special" reference letter for "chosen" coaches is extremely advantageous. It gives you another form of correspondence, and really demonstrates your personal influence on other golfers, their parents, and the junior golf world, in general. Be very discriminate on which coaches' you choose for this particular reference letter.

A sample thank you email is below:

To: coachb@xyzu.edu
From: student@home.com

Hi Coach B:

Thank you for taking the time to show me and my [mom or dad] around XYZ's campus and discuss your golf program. I was particularly interested in *[input some specifically interesting points about the golf program]*. XYZ University and your golf program have a great deal to offer student-athlete's and I am extremely interested in pursuing your program further.

Again, thank you for all of your time and effort, and I look forward to hearing from you soon. Please feel free to contact me at anytime.

Sincerely,

If you really believe this is a top choice, then add a paragraph discussing how you fit in and can contribute, such as:

After such an informative visit and further research, I feel that XYZ University, and your golf team, are at the top of my list of college choices. My grades and tournament average fit perfectly with your university and golf program. This environment is exactly what I am looking for, and I know I would be a valuable contributing asset to your team. I will call you next week to discuss my interests.

Again, thank you for all of your time and effort. Please feel free to contact me at anytime.

Sincerely,

Your Name
Your Cell Phone Number
Your Email Address

Keep a detailed list (refer back to our section on **"Choosing the Right College(s) for You"** for an example of spreadsheet headers and suggestions for your list) of the coaches who have received your information. Update it regularly with which components coaches have received, whom you have heard from, and notes on your impressions and conclusions regarding specific schools and/or coaches. Part of the marketing process is narrowing down your choices; keep yourself consistently apprised of where you feel you stand with coaches, and how you feel about different universities.

Coaches are hoping to have their offers extended, and verbally accepted during the summer. This is your time to really push hard on your marketing. Keep in constant contact with coaches, through email and phone calls, visiting campuses, sending reference letters, thank you notes, regular tournament updates, etc. If it's after July 1 after your junior year (for Div I, after June 15 for Div II), coaches can call you, don't let a call go unanswered.

We are fully aware that this is also an extremely busy time for you; trying to manage your complex tournament schedule, perform at your optimum ability, practice golf, market yourself, visit schools, speak to coaches, possibly hold down a job, etc. You can become notably frazzled and stressed. Take some time each day to focus and stay organized, use the calendars and to do lists you've set up to keep you on track. Also, take some time for yourself each day to have some fun, and/or spend some quiet time alone. It is important to stay stress free and focused.

By August, you should have your choices narrowed down to about 5-10 schools, with viable interest from each coach. Evaluate where you stand with each school, academically, athletically, and aesthetically. If you feel a school will be too much of a reach for you, it's time to knock it off the list. If you feel a school just doesn't have the right look and feel, it's time to knock it off the list. If you don't feel you have the right chemistry with a coach, it's time to knock it off the list. At this point, narrowing to a handful of choices is your goal.

WHEN TO SEND YOUR INFORMATION

Choose your top five and make a concerted effort to visit or revisit those schools. Make appointments with the coach before you visit the campus (always contact a coach to schedule time before your visit), even if you've already visited him/her before. Clearly state to the coach that you are extremely interested in his/her university, and would like to know what his/her scholarship opportunities are, and where you stand as a candidate for his/her team. Be extremely proactive, and let coaches know you are ready to make a decision. If you are physically unable to visit the campus, then call or email a coach conveying the same information.

It is better to receive an, "I'm sorry, but you are not one of my choices for a team member," than no answer at all. While this may be very disappointing, it gives you the opportunity to reexamine your list and your choices, and move forward. It also narrows your list further, without any effort on your part. Remember, you can only attend *one* school.

If, by mid-August, you have not received any offers, or are unhappy with the offer(s) you have received, go through the list again. Yes, again – this is a constantly repetitive process and can become quite tiring, draining, and overwhelming; but stay persistent and you will reap the benefits of all of your hard work.

Broaden your list and really take a long, hard look at every college you've been working with, and those you've never heard from, and those you never sent to. Resend a condensed version of your information to those you've sent to before, request scholarship and candidacy input from those you've been working with, and send your information to viable coaches you've never sent to before.

Once your senior classes begin, if you haven't accepted a verbal offer, and are offered an official visit by a coach – schedule it immediately, November signing is around the corner. It is always a good indicator that you are on a coach's possible recruit list when you receive an offer for an official visit. See our section on **"Visiting Colleges"** for more in depth information on official and unofficial visits.

Once the November signing is completed, if you have not signed – **DON'T PANIC** – plenty of opportunities still exist!! This is the ideal time to resend your information all over again to all of the coaches on your broadened list. Plan on sending your information after the Thanksgiving break and before the college's December exam week; this is perfect timing.

If coaches are looking, they have time to examine your information, and if they've filled their spots, they will, more than likely, let you know. At this point, we advise sending the new condensed version of your mailing. An email stating you are still interested in their school with your resume AND your swing video is recommended; short and to the point. They have just gone through hundreds of lengthy cover letters, resumes, and swing videos, maybe including yours – be brief during this contact, but full of critical information. Several coaches mentioned that it was during this second communication with our son, when his swing video and resume really caught their attention.

During this second (or third) wave, coaches and students don't have a lot of time to waste, and both are anxious to finalize their choices. This may very well be your best time to get recruited. Accept official visit offers, and really stay extremely focused on your follow ups and communications. Never let a phone call or email go unanswered.

By winter of your senior year, you should have just a few very interested coaches with offers on the table. It is time to make the all important final decision. Carefully review, examine, and discuss before you commit. See our section on **"Offers, Finances and Signings"** for further information regarding offers and your final decision.

WHEN TO SEND YOUR INFORMATION

RECAP

Winter/Spring (Junior Year)
- Send Resume and Cover Letter early December and/or early second semester of your Junior Year
- Send Swing Video April/May of your Junior Year
- Follow up with grades, awards, tournament finishes, etc.
- Send upcoming summer tournament schedule, end of your Junior Year
- Respond immediately to coaches who contact you
- Follow up every week or two with tournament updates and any other significant information

Summer (After Junior Year)
- Schedule unofficial visits around your summer tournaments
- Send thank you notes to coaches after visits
- Send golf reference letters to coaches
- Never let a phone call, email, or offer go unanswered
- Follow up every week or two with tournament updates
- Narrow your list and request scholarship and candidacy information from coaches
- Reevaluate, resend, follow up...reevaluate, resend, follow up

Fall (Senior Year)
- Once your senior year begins accept offers for official visits
- If you still haven't signed in November – begin again
- Begin applying to colleges
- Whittle your list

Winter/Spring (Senior Year)
- Send a condensed version of your information in early December
- Accept official visit offers
- Follow up weekly with updates on school and tournaments
- Do not let any communication from any coach go unanswered
- Stay on top of your correspondence right up until the April signing
- Make a final decision
- Accept and decline offer(s)

How to Send Your Information

There are basically two ways to send your information, email or postal mail:

While sending your information via **postal mail** is much more tangible, and literally gets the information into the coach's hands, it is also time delayed and cumbersome. Remember, you are not the only one sending information to a coach; there are more than likely, hundreds of letters and resumes sitting on a coach's desk. Many coaches have expressed their preference for email over postal mail, as their postal correspondence tends to pile up and sit on their desk for long stretches. However, If you choose to send your package via postal mail – make it stand out!

Just sending coaches your letter and resume in a plain envelope will not get your information on the top of their pile. Take some extra time to put your information in a pocket folder with your name and contact information on the front. Prepare a vibrant, professional package by choosing a new, bright colored folder with a label on the front, or have folders imprinted with your information on the front. When choosing your folder and envelope color, choose a vibrant, tasteful color, which stands out.

ALWAYS make sure each piece is typed, not handwritten, in a simple, easy to read font and sign your cover letter in black ink. Print your cover letter and resume on heavy, very bright white paper – do not use inexpensive, low weight paper. Place your cover letter in the left side of the folder pocket and your resume in the right pocket. This way, when opened, all of your pertinent information is easily identifiable, and laid out handily in front of the coach. This also creates an instant file on you, for the coach.

Sending your information via **email** is cost effective, immediate, and very widely used today. We highly recommend beginning your initial contact via email. As we stated earlier, most coaches commented that this is definitely their preferred method of communication.

| TIP | Always use a "professional" email address, such as JohnDoe@gmail.com; not something like nuttigolfr4u@ru.com.

Again, send your cover letter and resume in one email as your first contact to a coach. We advise putting your name, address, and contact phone number as your header to the cover letter email, in a slightly different font and/or color.

Sending your resume as an attachment, or as a continuation to the email, are both effective. However, the less work a coach has to do to retrieve your information, the better. Adding your resume to the bottom of the cover letter email, with an obvious break (such as a border line), takes less effort to view.

If you have initiated contact via email and have received a coach's email response, then this is obviously their preferred manner of communication. If after several email attempts, you do not receive an email response, then this is the time to send your information via postal mail, to get that particular coach's attention. Not all coach's respond to email, use your discretion as to when/how to send your follow up information.

Sending your swing video can be a complicated process. Of course, if going the postal route, copy it to DVD and send it in a hard envelope made for sending DVDs/CDs. There are more efficient, immediate, and cost effective routes you can take. It is preferable to utilize Social Media sites, send as an attached media file to an email, and/or create your own website to include your swing video.

Sending your swing video as an attached media file is often risky, because you are unaware of what software the coach may or may not have to view your video. Often coaches' use their time at tournaments to review future candidates' information on their phones, and an attached media file can make their phone viewing cumbersome.

Recruiters will frequently recommend a website to distribute your information. Coaches need very quick easy access, as their time is limited. Websites can often come across as pretentious and self-indulgent, with too many steps to evaluate a junior golfer's pertinent information. If you feel you must create your own website, make it extremely simple with your resume and swing video readily available on your front page. Resist the temptation to design an over the top, elaborate website, which only complicates the many steps a coach must take to review your relevant information.

There are many websites out there that offer junior golfer's the ability to upload their resume information and swing videos for a price; claiming their site is *the* site most often used by coaches for finding potential recruits. We have found this is simply untrue – most coaches rely heavily on direct contact from potential candidates, and rarely search the different recruiting websites.

We highly recommend using Social Media sites, such as YouTube, which are easy to use, cost effective (free of charge), and reach a broad audience. These sites simplify the distribution of your swing video, as you can simply include a link to the video in any emails sent to coaches. This also lets the coach know that your video will be seen by many other coaches, which can often be an incentive for them to contact you.

YouTube can accept most any video format, but here are some recommendations:

- Video Format: H.264, MPEG-2 or MPEG-4 are preferred
- 4:3 or 16:9 aspect rations are acceptable (without letterboxing)
- Resolution: 640x360 (16:9) or 480x360 (4:3) recommended, while 640x480 is also acceptable
- Audio Format: MP3 or AAC is preferred
- 30 Frames per second
- 5 minute maximum length

This may also be the time to begin calling coaches. While they, most likely, cannot return your call (check the NCAA guidelines on when coaches can contact you), if this is a school you are extremely interested in, call. You may very well get the coach on the line – be

HOW TO SEND YOUR INFORMATION

prepared to discuss your interests and qualifications, and ask to schedule an on campus visit with the coach.

Any way you choose to send your information, we can't express enough how important it is to follow up regularly and personally. We've heard many times that coaches want personalization; they don't want to contend with recruiters – they want to deal with you, personally. Email and phone calls, are, of course your best route for regular follow ups; however, utilize postal mail when necessary.

The Recruiting Process

While we wouldn't presume to have full knowledge about the recruiting process, we have learned quite a bit during our research, interviews, and discussions. Precisely how a coach goes about determining their best fit candidates, is unique to each coach.

Doing your part during the recruiting process is paramount. Always be professional, personal, well groomed, knowledgeable about their team and school, knowledgeable about your skill level, and above all, enthusiastic and modest (do not come across as arrogant). Know the rules before beginning the recruiting process, download the "NCAA Guide for the College-Bound Student-Athlete" at www.ncaastudent.org. See our section on **"Know the Governing Organizations"** for more in depth information.

In general, we have found that most coaches have a systematic approach when viewing a potential candidate's information. First, they look at your tournament scoring average and handicap. Next they turn their attention to your national tournament scores and finishes, and higher level high school tournaments such as, regional and state tournaments. They also like to see what kind of competition was in the field, and how many players were at your tournaments.

Once they have a good idea of your tournament play and you've gotten their attention, next they focus on your grades and standardize test scores. If your grades are not on par with their school's average, they will, more than likely, not take a second look, unless you are a spectacularly talented golfer. Lastly, they like to see what kind of person and athlete you are. They will look at your other sports (often they are looking for a good all around athlete), your job(s), volunteer work, and other interests. If you have peaked their interest, they will want to see you play and/or want to see your swing video.

While the recruiting process is all new to you, coaches go through the same routine every year – each in their own way. When visiting a coach, ask questions about their recruiting process to gain knowledge for your next visit. The recruiting process is quite one sided. Most likely, you are new to the process, and the college coach has to be a consummate professional at recruiting. Coaches are required to be extremely up to date on all of the rules and regulations in their division. While the vast majority of coaches take pride in their recruiting process and stay true to the established rules, there are always a few who may not present information appropriately. Pay close attention to what is being said and promised to you, and **always** ask if something doesn't seem right. The rules are in place to protect you, and you have the right to question any procedures that seem inappropriate.

Generally speaking, the larger, highly ranked schools, usually have a considerable recruiting budget. Therefore, head coaches are able to have others reviewing information, traveling to junior tournaments, watching swing videos, etc. Although, schools with a smaller recruiting budget are very efficient in reviewing talented junior golfers, and the advantage is that you will, more than likely, have contact with the head coach at all times.

The heaviest recruiting period is during the summer months; colleges are not in session and the coach's golf season is over. Coaches have a lot more time to focus on recruiting during this time, and your communication is key.

June through August is when most of the well known national tournaments occur, and you can be assured that many college coaches will be at these tournaments to view junior golfers.

Coaches commonly have a list of which players are on the board, and decide who to watch that day. Having your name and schedule in a coach's hands before the summer tournaments is essential to being noticed. They will often watch the field practicing on the range, and choose a few golfers to watch that particular day. Don't be surprised if a coach ends up following you for many holes – they really want to see you play in an intense tournament environment.

During the summer months, coaches are narrowing down their choices – they may ask you to visit their school for an unofficial visit after they see you play in a tournament (See our section on **"Know the Governing Organizations"** for details on when and how coaches can contact you, and official/unofficial visit guidelines). Jump on these opportunities, even if it isn't a school you had previously thought about as an option. Each time you meet with a new coach and visit a new school, you gain more knowledge about colleges, golf teams, and the recruiting process.

It is typical that coaches are looking for one to two (this is not to say that some coaches are not looking for more) players to fill their roster. Most coaches prefer to have their "picks" by mid to end of the summer, and present verbal offers. They will commonly whittle their choices down to about eight to ten players, and extend offers to their top picks. If declined, they will work their way through the choice players they had been working with during the summer.

A coach would love nothing more than to have his choice candidates signed in November and be done with this year's recruiting. However, it rarely works this way. A coach can have his top ten, extend offers, and not receive one verbal acceptance through August to October. Or worse, have verbal acceptances from his top two candidates, and neither actually sign in November.

So, don't give up if you haven't received an offer by the end of the summer – gear up! Really push your information out there right up until the beginning of early signing. You never know, a coach's top picks may have declined their offer just days before the early signing, and you may be next on their list.

August through the end of October is an extremely busy period for coaches. School is back in session and they are busy with their own teams and tournaments, in addition to recruiting and finalizing their choices for early signing. Don't be put off if you don't hear back from a coach right away – just keep updating them. We were surprised to hear from a coach at one of the smaller schools, that he had physically interviewed (that means a visit to his campus) over fifty potential candidates during that year! Imagine how many he had corresponded with, and how many resumes and swing videos he had seen and read. Coaches evaluate hundreds of junior golfers. Keep yourself in front of them and stand out.

Once the early signing period is over in November, every coach takes a deep breath. Some coaches may have gotten all of their signees, and are finished for now (see our section on **"Offers, Finances and Signings"** for more in depth information on offers and signings). However, as we've mentioned before, many, many candidates do not sign, even after accepting a verbal offer, for one reason or another.

Often coaches have to begin all over again, just like you. Coaches usually begin again by checking in on their other "top picks" they had been working with over the summer, to see if they are still available and interested. It is not uncommon for all of these candidates to be unavailable, as they have now signed with another team or decided to look elsewhere.

November through March is commonly off season for college golf, with minimal practices and no scheduled tournaments. Coaches have more time to evaluate and consider new candidates, but are anxious to have their following year's team in order. As we said before, be brief when sending these second (or third) packages, but full of information.

During this period, coaches will quickly offer potential candidates an official visit – jump at the chance if you feel their school may be a good fit (See NCAA Guidelines for rules and timing on official visit offers). Some coaches may discuss a possible scholarship dollar range prior to your visit. If a coach doesn't mention athletic

THE RECRUITING PROCESS

scholarship information, then ask, before accepting an official visit offer. They know you are hopeful for a scholarship, and neither you nor they have time to waste at this point.

Coaches like to have their upcoming fall team finalized by March. The regular signing period begins in mid-April, and they would like nothing more than to have their fall team complete, and move forward with their spring season. With persistence, it is likely that by mid-April, you will be signing with one of those teams!

According to NCAA Division I and II rules: A prospective student-athlete may make official visits beginning the opening day of their senior year. They can make one official visit per college, up to a maximum of five visits to separate colleges. Prior to an official visit, a prospective student-athlete is required to provide the college with a copy of their SAT, ACT or PLAN scores, NCAA Eligibility Center ID number, and Division I requires a copy of the prospective student-athlete's high school transcript.

Social Networking and Conduct

As we stated over and over, it is imperative that you consistently conduct yourself in a respectful manner, at all times. With the advent of social networking sites such as Facebook, MySpace, Twitter, Texting, etc., a teen's private life becomes very public quite quickly. Of course, you can always choose not to participate in any of this type of social networking, but that would be like building a bubble around you and sucking all of the fun out! A more sensible approach is to follow a few simple guidelines, and always remember your goal of playing college golf.

- Be discerning of who you accept as "friends" onto your site. You will want to make sure that your "friends" are a good reflection of what you represent.

- Be careful of your language and the language of others. Watch what is written on your wall, and what you write on others' walls. If someone is consistently disrespectful and uses inappropriate language on your wall, you will want to drop them as a "friend."

- Pay close attention to what is on your "friend's" sites as their sites become a reflection of you, by association. If you feel their information does not appropriately reflect your image, then drop them as a "friend."

- Be very discriminate on the pictures you post anywhere on the web. The minute you post a picture, it becomes public and out there for anyone's viewing. We've seen plenty of teens become entangled in a damaging web simply from a poor decision on a picture(s) they chose to post. Be very careful here, and scrutinize each of your photo postings by viewing them from an adult's eyes.

- By the same token, pay very close attention to the photos posted by others, on their sites. Watch for inappropriate photos of you, and request they be taken off their site. Also, pay close attention to photos of them on their site, other's sites, and your site. If you are the least bit wary of the photos they have on their site (even if they don't include you), then drop them as a "friend."

- Be conscious of who you choose to follow on Twitter, and the general overall sound of their tweets. If it is constantly full of inappropriate language and/or photos, then stop following them.

- Without a doubt, texting has become one of the greatest instantaneous forms of communication. Always remember, that someone is receiving each text or photo you send from your phone. Be careful of what you send – think twice, and just simply *don't*, if it is the least bit unacceptable by social standards. Also remember, that texts are kept with your phone company and can be pulled and printed, if needed.

Be conscious of the image you portray, and look at your sites and texting with a questioning eye. This will serve you well in the long run, and eliminate any chance of questions later on.

SOCIAL NETWORKING & CONDUCT

Coaches are always checking and talking to each other. Present a stellar image at all times, during recruiting and after. Once you have an offer, don't give a coach any reason to question their choice.

Example of a Postal Cover Letter Header:

Date

University Name
Attn: Coach's Full Name
Department of Athletics Golf Program
University Address
Specific Coach's Building or Mail Stop Address (if you have it)
Town, State Zip Code

Dear Coach [Coach's Last Name]:

Examples of an Email Cover Letter Header:

Your Name
Your Street Address
Your Town, State Zip Code
Your Email Address
Your Phone Information

> *You may want to add a classic color (such as navy) to your header to have it stand out*

Dear Coach [Coach's Last Name]:

University Name   *Your Name*
Attn: Coach's Full Name   *Your Street Address*
Town, State Zip Code   *Your Email Address*
                                                   Your Phone Information
                                                   Your Town, State Zip Code

Dear Coach [Coach's Last Name]:

> *Dates are not necessary when using email as the email itself provides a date – however, this is your decision on whether to add it or not.*
>
> *Professionalism and personalization are the keys here.*

COVER LETTER & RESUME EXAMPLES

Examples of Cover Letter:

Dear Coach [Coach's Last Name]:

Choose your email or postal header.

My name is [your name] and I am a [your grade] at [your high school name] in [your town, state]. I am extremely interested in attending and playing golf at [University Name]. Through many years of hard work and discipline, I am prepared to take my golf skills to the next level.

[Your High School Name] is a [your UIL level] District UIL school and competes amongst [decide here how to describe your school's competition level]. Since my junior year, I have been first on [your high school name] Varsity team, broken school records, placed 2nd personally in District, helped take our team to 2nd Team All-District, and won two tournaments. The most recent tournament I won a few weeks ago in bitter cold and high wind conditions at [Golf Resort in Town, State], with a two day score of 144. Additionally, our team took first place in that tournament. I have finished in the top ten in 5 out of our 6 high school tournaments, thus far this season.

I currently play in a variety of tournaments, among foremost junior golfers, including [include a brief list of the upper level tour groups you play in]. This past week, I won a two day tournament during a [insert junior tour name] at [Golf Resort in Town, State], with a two day total of 142 (69-73); winning the tournament by 6 strokes. I have succeeded in placing in the top 5-10 in many of these tours (including a number of wins), and this summer I plan on qualifying for more National tournaments and developing my skills to the next level.

My GPA after the end of my first semester this school year is [GPA] out of 4.0. I made the academic honor roll this past year and am on track to graduate with honors. I work part time at [job name] and enjoy diverse social, volunteer, and recreational activities, which are further explained in my golf resume.

After reviewing your college's academics and golf team statistics [give some specifics here to show you've done your research on their University], I am confident I can be a significant asset to [University Name's] Varsity Golf Team beginning in [year of your freshman attendance to college].

Below is my golf resume, which highlights my golf, academic, work, and volunteer achievements. In a couple of weeks, I will be sending my golf swing video online, please look for it in your inbox. I appreciate your time in reviewing my information.

Thank you for consideration and I look forward to hearing from you soon.

Sincerely,

[Your Name]

This letter is an excellent representation of the type of information you want to portray in your letter. Pick and choose the pieces of this letter, which fit you best, and pull it together in a concise one page correspondence.

It includes a great deal of information. It quickly and briefly introduces you, highlights a couple of your outstanding tournaments, which tours you play in, your academic information, and other interests/activities.

It is personalized towards that specific coach and their institution, and is respectful and professional. It points the coach towards your resume and indicates another follow up communication with more information.

Of course, you should research a variety of cover letters, and use your own words to create an exemplary cover letter, suited to you.

COVER LETTER & RESUME EXAMPLES

Example of Golf Resume

[Your Name]

Personal Information:

Address:	[Your Address]
Home/Cell Phone:	[Your Cell Phone]
Email Address:	[Your Email]
Birth Date:	[Your Birth Date]
Parent's Name(s):	[Your Parent's Name(s)]
Parent Cell Phone:	[Your Parent's Cell Phone]
Parent Email:	[Your Parent's Email]

Face Front Photo of You

High School Information:

High School:	[High School Name and Address]
High School Coach:	[High School Coach's Name & Phone]
Graduation Date:	[Month, Year]
Current Grade:	[Your Current Grade]
GPA:	[Your GPA]
SAT:	[Your SAT]
ACT:	[Your ACT]
HS Scoring Average:	[HS Scoring Avg/9 holes; Name of Golf Club]
USGA GHIN:	[Handicap (GHIN Number)]
Tournament Avg:	[Your Tournament Scoring Average]
Home Golf Course:	[Name, Address, and Phone Number]

Competition Highlights:

Date	Location/Course	Tour/Tournament	Score	Finish
Include Date(s) of Tournament	Include Name of Course; Town, State; On the next line include Yardage / Par / Rating / Slope; On the next line include Weather Conditions.	Include Name of Tour and Tournament. On the next couple of lines include any important information such as Qualified, Strong Nationally Ranked Field, etc.	Your Score for each day and total overall score.	Your finish / total amount of players in field.

Upcoming Schedule:

Date	Location/Course	Tour/Tournament
Include Date(s) of Tournament	Include Name of Course; Town, State; Phone Number	Include Name of Tour and Tournament.

High School Awards / Achievements:

Freshman [Year]: List academic and athletic achievements.
Sophomore [Year]: List academic and athletic achievements.
Junior [Year]: List academic and athletic achievements.
Senior [Year]: List academic and athletic achievements.

Interests / Activities / Volunteer Work:

List other athletic interests, activities, job(s), and volunteer work.

References:

Name	Name
Title	Title
Location	Location
Street Address	Street Address
Town, State, Zip	Town, State, Zip
Phone Number	Phone Number
Email Address	Email Address

> *You will be able to format your resume well on appropriate size paper. But, overall, this resume is professional and reflects all of the information needed in a good solid resume.*
>
> *You will want to include 10-15 of your top Competition Highlights, with as much information as possible.*
>
> *Don't go too far out with your upcoming schedule; keep it to the following month or two, depending on how many tournaments you have scheduled.*

www.ACollegeGolfPlan.com

Chapter 5

Visiting Colleges

We've spent a great deal of time talking about coach's standards and college's criteria, but in the end, this is really all about you, the individual. This is about how **you** feel about your chosen university and how well suited **you** are to the university and the team, but also how well suited they are to **you**. Colleges and coaches will see hundreds, if not thousands, of students come and go over the years; each student being unique in their own right and leaving a little piece of themselves behind, and taking a piece of their university with them. It is your choice and your decision; it must be what is right for **you**, not someone else. Your final choice must elicit a passion and comfort towards the school. Visiting colleges is **the single most valuable element** in your long search. It is often the determining factor in your final decision amongst colleges.

Keep in mind that this will be your new home and your new family for the next four years. More than likely, it will be your first time living away from your family and taking care of yourself on a daily basis. When meeting coaches, their families, and their teams, assess whether you feel really comfortable with them and your surroundings. Would you be proud and comfortable saying I go to "XYZ University" and this is "my team"?

That being said, there is a college out there for everyone and not just one. Just like, there is not just one perfect home or just one perfect car. As we grow and change, so do our ideas and viewpoints about our environment and ourselves. Again, when visiting colleges keep an open mind and really take in the atmosphere around you – is it where you belong?

We presented a list of questions to ask yourself in the chapter on **"Choosing the Right College(s) for You,"** this is the time to look those over again and reevaluate your answers. If your ideas have changed, then adjust your answers. Study these questions and your answers before and after each visit, and adjust them as needed. Take them with you on your visits (along with our questions outlined in this chapter); they are elemental to finding out what is important to you and which school/team is best suited to you.

For every student, visiting a college is a critical stage in the process of finding the right fit for you; but for the student-athlete, the process is heightened and there are many more facets to each visit. You are not only evaluating the campus, the degree programs, the dorms, the classrooms, the café's, the recreational centers, etc., but the junior golfer is also appraising the coach, the team, the athletic facilities, the courses, the team schedule and more. Keeping track of all of these different moving parts can seem overwhelming. Staying organized, taking good notes, asking a lot of questions, taking photographs, reviewing your own questions, and maintaining a good up to date list will keep you on target.

For student-athlete's there are two types of college visits, "unofficial" and "official." In the next section, we go into more detail about each type of visit, and set forth a good approach to managing your visits. Additionally, at the end of this chapter, we include a new set of questions for you to ask a coach, questions you may be asked by a coach, and questions you may want to ask existing team members.

Unofficial and Official Visits – What to Expect

The following information is based on the overall NCAA Guidelines, which you should research at www.ncaa.org, as each Division may have specific guidelines. It is a good idea to stay abreast of these guidelines during visits and communications with coaches.

An unofficial visit is defined as visits made by you at your own expense (see the NCAA Guidelines for in depth information on the guidelines for each Division). A student-athlete can take an unlimited amount of unofficial visits to colleges anytime before, and including, their senior year. College coaches are allowed to meet and speak with you, as long as the meeting takes place on campus.

Additionally, high schools often allow a certain number of days per year or per semester for juniors and/or seniors to take for college visits, without attendance consequences. Check with your college career center and/or your counselor to see how many days your school allows, and what paper work is required before/after your visit. Often a coach or admissions officer will have to sign your high school college visit paperwork during your visit.

Take advantage of your tournament travel to visit schools while you are away. This is an excellent use of your time before and/or after your tournaments. Before you leave for a tournament, research the colleges that are in the surrounding area of the tournament site and schedule a visit(s).

Always schedule a campus tour (you can do this on the school's website or by calling the college admissions office). Campus tours are typically conducted by upper-class college students who have intimate knowledge of the school. The tour guides have been through a training process to thoroughly acquaint them with the finer points and history of the school. The tours often include other interested high school students and their parents, giving you the advantage of discovering new information through other students questions. Coaches readily admit that a campus tour, with a trained tour guide, is a far better way to thoroughly learn about the campus, rather than a tour with the coach.

UNOFFICIAL AND OFFICIAL VISITS

Count on campus tours taking at least 1 ½ hours or more and be on time. They commonly leave from the admissions office, tour the entire campus, and return to the admissions office. It's difficult to "catch up" once the tour has left the admissions office. Some will have a question and answer session with a professor or dean, while others will not. If there is a certain building you wish to see that doesn't appear to be included in the tour, simply ask the tour guide and, if they are permitted, they will gladly accommodate your request. Tour guides are extremely informative and give you an excellent overall view of the school.

We do not recommend trying to visit more than one school per day. Once you find your way to the campus and the admissions office, the tour usually lasts 1 ½ hours or more, and you will typically want to look around a bit yourself afterwards. This takes nearly a half to full day, in itself. Additionally, colleges aren't often very close together and it becomes difficult and tiring, trying to race from one school to the next.

When choosing which schools to visit, compare the schools to those on your list. If the schools around your tournament(s) are not potential candidates on your list, visit at least one anyway. With each visit, you gain more knowledge about colleges and coaches. Determining what kind of school you want to attend is often challenging, and college visits are significant in helping you better understand what type of campus environment is right for you.

We recommend beginning to visit colleges in the second semester of your sophomore year, right through your senior year, if necessary. Starting in your sophomore year, gives you time to review a few schools, without the pressure of college golf. This is the time to simply take some tours and look around, giving you an idea of what you like and don't like in a campus environment.

Visit colleges in your junior year including both a campus visit and a meeting with the golf coach, if you are able to schedule one. Call or email the coach a few weeks, or more, prior to your visit to check his/her availability. If you call a coach *before* July 1 *after* your junior year, he/she cannot call you back (see NCAA

Guidelines). Email or continue to call until you get him/her on the line. If you haven't sent your letter and resume to the coaches on your list yet, do so before you visit a particular school/coach.

Remember, coaches can contact you via phone, after July 1 for NCAA Division I, and after June 15 for NCAA Division II, of your junior year.

If you are able to schedule time with the coach, let him/her know what time your campus tour is, to coordinate around the tour. When meeting with a college coach, dress neatly and appropriately, be respectful and interactive. The coach will likely meet with you in his/her office to discuss their golf programs, and find out about you.

This is the time to learn everything you can about the coach, his/her coaching style, golf program, team, etc. You and your parent(s) should go armed with a series of relevant questions. The coach will also ask you questions about your interests in the school, his/her golf program, your other interests and activities, your golf and more (see our list of questions at the end of this chapter). He/she will likely want to show you their golf facilities, both on and off campus, if they are close by. This is a very valuable time to learn all you can about this school's golf program, and to make a good impression on the coach.

An official visit is defined as a college visit fully or partially paid for by the university, and the length of the visit may not exceed 48 hours (see the NCAA guidelines for more in depth information). Official visits can only be offered to seniors after the start of their senior year. A prospective student-athlete is only allowed five official visits to five separate institutions during their senior year. Typically, during an official visit, a university will pay for your transportation to/from the school, your meals during your stay and your lodging (which is commonly staying with a team member on campus). An accompanying parent(s) can also be offered paid expenses (check the NCAA Guidelines for these specifications and check with the coach).

UNOFFICIAL AND OFFICIAL VISITS

According to NCAA Division I and II rules: A prospective student-athlete may make official visits beginning the opening day of their senior year. They can make one official visit per college, up to a maximum of five visits to separate colleges. Prior to an official visit, a prospective student-athlete is required to provide the college with a copy of their SAT, ACT or PLAN scores, NCAA Eligibility Center ID number, and Division I requires a copy of the prospective student-athlete's high school transcript.

If you have already received and accepted a verbal offer from a coach prior to your senior year, he/she may still offer you an official visit once school begins. It is a good idea to attend an official visit after you've accepted a school's offer. By participating in an official visit, you'll have the ability to spend time with the team and be treated to a couple of days of "college life," which can build your confidence and chemistry with the coach and team. If you were only able to visit the university and coach over the summer, visiting again in the fall gives you a whole new perspective, students are back on campus, the golf team is back in school, and classes are in session.

If you haven't accepted a verbal offer before commencing your senior year, and a college coach offers you an official visit, this is an excellent opportunity. College coaches work within a strict recruiting budget. Being offered an official visit is often an excellent sign that a particular coach is interested in you as a potential team member. An invitation by a coach to visit his/her college is different from an unofficial visit, in that the visit is driven by the coach, instead of you. Most of your expenses are typically paid for, and, more than likely, you will have an opportunity to stay with a team member in the dorms and eat on campus.

Do your research before attending an official visit. Investigate the website to be prepared with pertinent questions and check into their campus tour scheduling. Often, an official visit includes a weekday and weekend day. Arrange your timing with the coach to include plenty of weekday time for a campus tour, time to see classrooms in session, and time with an admissions and/or financial officer, etc. Plan your travel time efficiently to maximize seeing all you can during your visit.

An official visit can be anywhere from a laid back visit to a highly organized, agenda driven visit. Either way, a coach will likely schedule you for a campus tour, a meeting with an admissions officer and/or a financial aid officer, give you a guided tour of the golf facilities, and a discussion or two with you in his/her office. He/she will likely have you stay over at least one night on campus with a team member(s) in their dorm room, and provide you with meals on and off campus.

A coach may schedule some time for you to practice with the team; check with the coach to decide whether or not to bring your clubs. *According to NCAA guidelines, a college golf coach cannot watch you practice or play during a visit at their campus*, however, you can practice with the team members, without the coach in attendance. If there are any areas the coach doesn't cover, or buildings/classrooms you would like to see that weren't on the tour, take this opportunity to ask the coach.

Many coaches like to have a dinner out with you, your parent(s), an assistant coach (if they have one), themselves, and their spouse. This is a great interactive experience for all parties to enjoy themselves, and get to know each other on a more personal and social level.

As we've said numerous times, it is imperative to conduct yourself in a respectful manner. While on a visit, here are a few pointers to remember:

- Dress neatly and professionally. Always dress to impress. Make sure you and/or your parent(s) are not wearing clothing or other apparel from another university.

- Be on time! Do not leave a coach waiting. If you are traveling and are running late due to flight or traffic delay, call the coach and let him/her know. If you've arranged with the coach to call him/her when you land or make it into town, don't call five minutes before you arrive on campus – give him/her at least 20 minutes notice.

- Be honest about your golf talent – don't over exaggerate; the coach has surely checked your records by now.

- Be interactive and proactive. Ask questions, join in discussions, and ask for clarifications.

- Don't just ask questions about the athletic program; ask about the academics, the dorms, the food, and other programs.

- Do not speak poorly about other coaches or other universities. Coaches know each other and keep in touch; they talk.

- Complement his/her program, the university, and other aspects about the area.

- Parents should be cautious not to interrupt their teen or the coach. Allow the coach and your son/daughter to drive the conversation.

- If at the end of the visit, there hasn't been any discussion about scholarships or offers, don't blatantly ask if he/she wants to offer you a scholarship. The best way to handle this is to ask, "what is the next step"?

- Always, always, be extremely appreciative throughout your visit, but especially during your departure. Remember, a coach has taken a lot of time out his busy schedule to prepare for, and partake in, your visit! Use those please and thank you's you've grown up listening to all of these years!

Recruiting is an integral part of a coach's job, and they conduct many visits per year, year after year. Coaches are an excellent resource; ask a lot of questions. They prefer an interactive student who shows a great deal of interest in their school and program over the uninvolved, overly quiet student and/or parent. Be engaging, curious, and interactive during your time with the coach and team members. Remember, while they are assessing you, you are also assessing them, and their school.

So often, parents and prospective student-athletes forget that not only is a coach interviewing you; you are also interviewing the coach, and evaluating the school. While you are selling yourself, they are also selling you on their golf program and their university. As we said earlier, this decision is all about you – take the time to really evaluate everything you can about the school and their golf program.

Questions During Your Campus Visit

We've said it over and over again that, this decision is about you, and this should always be in the back of your mind when face to face with a potential coach. Be prepared with your list of questions, and be prepared to skillfully answer their questions. We've included a list of questions for you to ask during your interview, questions for you to be prepared to answer from a coach, and questions to ask team members.

During your time with the coach, there will be general interactive discussion throughout your visit. The coach will likely schedule time one on one with you and your parent(s) in his/her office. This is your time to shine and ask any unanswered questions. Being equipped with relevant questions, and prepared to answer questions in a mature, knowledgeable manner gives you an advantage over ill-prepared potential candidates. It is nearly impossible to anticipate a wild card question, but having the ability and knowledge base to respond intelligently, is always impressive. Do your research and go prepared.

It's possible that a coach will extend a verbal offer, or at least discuss the probability of an offer. Anticipate this discussion and be prepared with your questions and answers. It is advisable not to verbally accept any offer right on the spot – take time afterwards to digest all of the information, and discuss it with your parents to make a well informed decision.

Possible Questions From Coaches

* Why do you want to go to "XYZ University"?

* What interests you about our particular golf program?

* What are you planning to major in during your college years?

* What are your GPA, SAT and ACT scores?

* What other interests/activities do you participate in, both in and out of school?

* What do you feel are the strengths and weaknesses of your game?

* Are you working with a teaching professional? If so, who?

* How long have you been working with your teaching pro?

* Do you have different instructors for your swing, short game, etc.?

* What is your average practice routine like?

* What type of tournaments are on your upcoming schedule?

* What is your handicap?

* What is your plan after college; does it include attempting to play as a tour professional and/or a career in the golf world?

* Are you looking for a golf scholarship?

* Would you be willing to play without a golf scholarship?

* Do you and your parents know approximately what you would like to/are able to spend for college?

* Do you have other offers you are considering?

* Where do you stand in your college search process? How many other schools do you still have on your list to visit?

* When do you plan on making your final decision?

Questions To Ask A College Coach

- How long have you been coaching? How long at this university?

- How many students do you have on your team?

- How many players are you looking to recruit for my graduation year?

- How many, if any, players have you already signed this year?

- What is your tournament qualification process like?

- What conference does your school play in?

- What other teams are typically at your tournaments?

- How many teams compete at your tournaments?

- Does your school sponsor a tournament? If so, at what course?

- Do *all* of your players play in your sponsored tournament?

- When are your in-season and off-season times?

- When are the conference championships?

- How many individuals and/or teams move on to the NCAA (or other organizations) finals?

- How many tournaments do you play per year?

- What is a typical tournament travel schedule like?

- Do you take other trips outside of team tournament travel?

- How many days of school do your travel players miss per year?

- When are your practices during the week (what time and how often)?

- Do you have scheduled strengthening and cardio work out times? When are they?

- What's the difference in scheduled time in-season and off-season?

- What kind of rules do you have for your players?

QUESTIONS DURING YOUR VISIT

- What kind of academic support does your program offer? Tutors? Scheduling help?
- Do you have regularly scheduled study groups?
- What type of GPA levels do you expect from your players?
- What is your business (or whatever your academic major interest is in) program like?
- What is the student/teacher ratio in classes?
- Are freshman required to take a freshman seminar?
- Are you a fully funded program?
- How many scholarships do you offer per year?
- Where do you feel I fit into your possible recruits list?
- Do you think I would play my freshman year?
- Where do you think I would stand on your roster?
- What do you expect during holidays and summer?
- Do you schedule any college golf tournaments and/or practices during college holidays or breaks?
- Would I have to arrive earlier in the summer for practices, before classes begin?
- Do most of your team members live on campus?
- Do you know who I would be rooming with, if I attend my freshman year?
- What types of on and off campus activities do you permit?
- What brand of clubs/equipment do you typically use?
- Are you sponsored by a golf brand? If so, who?
- Can I use all of my own equipment, shoes, etc.?

Questions To Ask Team Members

* What brought you to "XYZ University"?

* Do you like it here?

* Do you like the other students and teachers? (overall atmosphere)

* What is the coaching staff like?

* Do you like the coaching staff? Why?

* What is the weather like?

* Do you like the practice course(s)?

* Do you like the indoor facilities?

* What is a typical daily schedule like for you?

* What is the travel like?

* How far away do you typically go to attend a tournament?

* How hard is it to keep up with your school work and golf schedule?

* Do you use the tutors, schedulers, and other people offered to help with school work and class organization?

* Are most of the professors good about athletes missing classes, etc. for travel?

* How hard/easy are the classes?

* How do you like the dorms/apartments?

* What is the food like?

* What do you do socially, during your free time?

* Do you hang out mostly together, or not?

QUESTIONS DURING YOUR VISIT

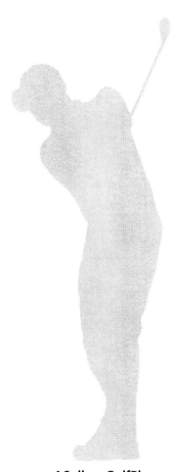

www.ACollegeGolfPlan.com

Chapter 6

Applying to Colleges

The physical act of applying to a college can seem quite intimidating. There are many components, which comprise a successful application. For the student-athlete, having a college coach behind you can help the process go more smoothly, however it also adds another element to the process.

Being prepared is the key to a successful application. We have outlined the different parts of the application process, and how to generate an exceptional college application.

The Application Process

* Most, if not all, high schools typically offer an evening presentation on applying to colleges. Attending one of these sessions will get you started on understanding the application process, and your specific high school requirements.

* When applying to a college, the best choice is to apply online if you can. If you have to apply to a college on paper, use a good black ink pen and ensure your handwriting is neat and readable. Make two copies of the application and use one as a draft.

* Many states now offer an online application that can be applied to any of their public schools. Often, the "state" application requires additional information for the specific school you are

applying to, such as an essay, references, etc. Check with the college for their specific requirements.

* All colleges require a "sealed" copy of your transcripts. Check with your high school to see if they do this electronically or manually. This process commonly requires a form and an adult's signature, and may take up to 48 hours to receive. Check with your high school counselor or registrar's office early in the fall of your senior year, to learn about your high school's sealed transcript procedures. Know this information early on, so you are not scrambling to make a college's deadline or a college coach's request.

* If your high school prints sealed transcripts manually, request several at once to have readily available to send to colleges. This will make it easier when the time comes to submit your application. *Remember, do not open them, they must remain sealed for a college to consider you.* However, it is a wise idea to request an additional one to review yourself, checking to make sure all of your information is correct.

* Frequently, college coaches may ask to have your transcript faxed to them for review, or they may need a copy as part of their "official" visit package requirements (see the NCCA guidelines regarding "official" visits). Coaches want to make sure they are receiving a complete package when looking at your qualifications. They want to ensure you are able to be admitted to their university, and your academics are on par with their institution's requirements. More than likely, you will have to fill out the same transcript request form at your high school to have your transcript faxed. High schools *can only* fax transcripts to an athletic director at a college; communicate to your high school that your transcript fax will be going *directly* to an athletic director at that college (request the coach's *direct* fax line). This *is not* a sealed transcript and cannot be used for admission into the school; a separate sealed transcript will need to be sent when formally applying to the admissions office of the college.

- Most colleges require a recommendation form to be submitted by your counselor. Print this form and ask your counselor for completion. Do this as soon as you know you are applying to that college. Counselors receive many recommendation form requests, and it may take some time for them to complete the information.

- Some colleges request an educational reference letter and some do not. It has been our experience that when applying, more is better (to a degree). Even if a college doesn't require an educational reference letter, it is best to send one. Remember those academic reference letters you've been gathering from teachers, counselors, and administrators – this is the time and place to use them! Don't overload them on reference letters; choose the best one, which represents you well, for that particular college.

- Send your SAT and ACT scores as soon as you've decided to apply to a college.

- You can send your SAT scores from www.collegeboard.com and your ACT scores from www.actstudent.org.

- Some schools accept your SAT and ACT scores electronically and others do not. How colleges accept these scores will often be displayed when you are requesting a copy to be sent to a school (if it is not displayed, call the college admissions office and ask how they receive SAT and ACT scores). If a college only receives them physically by mail, you may consider spending the extra money to have them sent express, particularly if you are trying to make a deadline for the school or the college coach.

- Nearly all colleges require some sort of essay or a series of short answer questions. We know that students dread this part of the application process, but a few good pointers and some individual help, can make this a much smoother and rewarding experience. The last section of this chapter addresses insights and guidance on the college essay.

THE APPLICATION PROCESS

- Nearly all colleges will supply you with a list of required documents to follow. Check off your documents as you put them into your packet, and double check again to verify you have properly completed each document and it is all in your package.

- When sending your application, often schools will ask for a declaration of what type of application you are submitting. We've defined some terms below that you will often see on applications and school websites, but always check with the school for their specific definition and deadline(s):

  ▶ *Regular Admission:* This is the traditional application, whereby a student can apply up to the regular deadline, and is notified at a specified time, usually around April 1 (deadlines vary by school; check with the school). If admitted, you are under no obligation to attend this college.

  ▶ *Early Action:* A student can submit an application early in their senior year, usually between October 30 and January 15, before the regular deadline, and is considered as soon as the application is received (check the school for deadlines). The answer usually takes up to two to four weeks after the application is received. If admitted, you are under no obligation to attend this college.

  ▶ *Early Decision:* A student can submit an application for their first choice school early in their senior year, between October 30 and January 15, and is considered as soon as the application is received (check the school for deadlines). The student and their guidance counselor must sign a contract with the school. *Early Decision requires a legal obligation to attend that school, if admitted. Do not confuse Early Action and Early Decision.* The answer usually takes up to two to four weeks after the application is received.

  ▶ *Rolling Admissions:* A student can submit their application at any time, and their application is reviewed immediately after it is received. They are often notified within a few weeks. Commonly, colleges with rolling admissions accept applications until spaces are no longer available (check the school's rules and deadlines). If admitted, you are under no obligation to attend this college.

* Make a copy of all of your paperwork before sending it to the institution. This will make it a lot easier should something happen between your home or computer, and their admissions offices.

When and Where To Apply

This may be a bit trickier than you think. Because you are attempting to secure a golf scholarship at a college institution, you will most likely seek guidance from your potential coach on when to apply. However, paying attention to college deadlines is an essential part of your planning process.

In the fall of your senior year, assess where you stand with potential coaches and colleges. If you are working with a particular coach(es), seek their advice on applying to their college. They may have a specific way they would like you to apply and/or a specific timeframe. However, research their college's academic scholarship and other deadlines, and make sure the coach is aware of these deadlines.

If your fall semester seems to be slipping by without direction from a coach towards applying to a college, then reevaluate your application strategy. It's a great idea to have a "back up" college(s) in your pocket, just in case. With deadlines looming, pick a college or two that you would love to attend, even if you don't play golf, and apply; and/or apply to the colleges on your golf "wish" list, which you feel are viable academic and athletic options. Applying to colleges can become costly, as each school usual requires a non-refundable application fee; there is typically a fee associated with sending sealed transcripts; and there are fees related to sending your SAT and ACT scores. Be prudent when choosing which applications to send.

WHEN & WHERE TO APPLY

You don't want to miss the deadline for applying to a college and you especially don't want to miss academic scholarship deadlines. Many college deadlines for academic scholarships are between December and January. And, even with a golf scholarship, you are still, more than likely, able to accept an academic scholarship (check with the institution's admissions or financial aid office regarding combining financial aid packages).

While our son had an excellent GPA and very good SAT/ACT scores, he was not a 4.0+ student, and we were pleasantly surprised when he received an academic scholarship from every school where he submitted an application. Academic scholarships are on a per school basis and each one has their own system for scholarship acceptance. Some even publish their numbers on their website, and often a phone call to admissions or financial aid will provide you with their system and numbers for academic scholarships. Most college "numbers" are normally a calculation of your GPA, SAT, and/or ACT scores compared with their existing incoming freshman applications. Other schools may use a more standardized ladder approach utilizing GPA, SAT, and/or ACT scores, without comparing these scores to incoming freshman applications. Always check with the school.

There may come a time when you've heard from a college coach at a new school that really excites you and fits you well, but it is after the academic scholarship deadline(s), or even possibly the overall application deadline. If this happens, let the coach know that you will be applying after the deadline(s), and feel you may also be a candidate for an academic scholarship. Often times, the coach can speak to the admissions office regarding the reasons behind your delayed application.

The College Essay

By no means are we experts on the college essay, but having been through the experience and sought advice from many sources, we can provide you with some fundamental ideas on the different types of essays, and what colleges are looking for in your essay writing.

Generally speaking, the point to a college essay is to identify potential students who are intelligent, and can write an interesting composition that sets them apart from others. Colleges want to know about you, your insights, your personality, how you view the world around you, if you do your research, and where you feel you fit in. Basically, everyone has a story, and colleges want to hear your story told in different ways through different experiences and/or influences. This isn't as monumental a task as you might think. Take your time and use your resources when putting together your college essay(s).

There are plenty of books and internet sites that offer information about, and samples of, college essays to assist you. Studying professor's comments and evaluations of sample essays can prove to be extremely beneficial. Use a parent, teacher, counselor, friend, and/or tutor to help you edit your essay(s), to present them as effectively as possible. Above all, do not plagiarize or have someone write them for you; this does not serve you or your potential college well, and colleges are fully aware of all of the sample essays readily available.

Always review your essays several times for spelling, grammar, and vocabulary.

There are basically four types of essays, which come in different forms of questions:

The About You / Significant Achievement Essay:
This may come in different types of questions, but overall they are looking for a focused description about you through an achievement or experience perspective. Typically, the idea is to show perseverance, growth, risk, reward, how your experiences changed you, how you've given back through your growth, what you've learned, and how you use that knowledge today to better yourself.

What colleges don't want is a list of your incredible accomplishments, or self-absorbed writing. Choose one experience or accomplishment and, in a non-arrogant fashion, describe how

THE COLLEGE ESSAY

you have been bettered by this experience. Tell your story through a mature perspective.

The Significant Issue / Hot Topic Essay:

This essay is usually asking your opinion on a national, political, or social issue. They are definitely looking for your view on an issue; however, they want to see that you can objectively see both sides of an issue, even if you stand on one side. Resist the temptation to be preachy or come across as a self centered "know it all." You'll want to portray your unique point of view, keeping in mind that there are two sides (or more) to every issue.

Know that you are not an expert on the subject and keep your writing within your own knowledge range. Assume that your audience knows more about this issue than you do; keep it personal and realistic.

Portray that you are aware of the world around you and that societal issues affect you and your life. Explain how your issue touches you personally, how it has changed you, why it is important to you, and what you have learned from studying this topic. Take time to present evidence for both sides of the subject matter to show that you are a thinker and a researcher, and have a good grasp on what goes on around you, and your part in society.

The Why Us / Why College Essay:

This essay is looking at your future goals and your commitment and dedication to higher education. Make a point of complimenting aspects of the school, while showing how their college can make a positive impact on you and, in turn, how you can make an impact on them.

Demonstrate some knowledge about the college. Do your research and choose specific aspects of the college that have made an impression on you, and have moved you towards their institution. Be honest and credible about your desire to attend this college, without sounding too overconfident or too ingratiating.

The Personal Influence Essay:

This essay is about **you**, while using experiences from another person; this is a vitally important aspect to your writing. Colleges are looking to hear about **you, your** story, **your** growth, and **your** commitment, not someone else's. This can be tricky to keep the reader engaged in your perspective, while describing another person's influence on you; you'll need to watch your tone.

Impress your audience with personal growth, what you've learned about yourself, your values, your sense of community, and your goals. Be honest and unpretentious – don't overuse "fancy" language thereby making it sound fake or contrived. Avoid the attraction to overwrite, making your experience, or the influential person you are describing, sound grandiose or greater than life. Be real and truthfully describe how this person helped mold you into who you've become today.

Many students choose one or both of their parents as their influential person(s), and admissions committees receive an overabundance of essays written about one's parent(s). The disadvantage to choosing a parent is the "cliché" aspect. However, the advantage is that you have a personal level of knowledge about your parent(s), making it easier to describe them and their affect on you. If you choose this route, be careful to stay on target talking about you, and how they have influenced you, rather than dwelling on your parent's enormous struggles and/or accomplishments.

Another trap to avoid is a barrage of over the top lists of your feelings and emotions towards this person. Be simple and to the point about how they, or their experiences, have influenced you.

Always, try to use a catchy first line to pull the reader in from the start, and pull it all together, in a few sentences, in your concluding paragraph. An organized essay that is well thought out from beginning to end is the ultimate goal.

THE COLLEGE ESSAY

Your essay(s) are a true reflection of who you are from the inside out. Show yourself through your writing to the admissions committee in a simple, honest fashion. In the end, this is what they are looking for, the true you showing through.

Chapter 7

Offers, Finances and Signings

You've, no doubt, heard or read the terms verbal offer, written offer, athletic scholarship, signed, full ride, need-based aid, non-need based aid, non-repayable financial aid, etc. during your college search. These terms can become overwhelming and bewildering.

It's important to understand these terms and use them to your advantage. We've outlined definitions and descriptions in this chapter to help you navigate your way through the terminology.

VERBAL AND WRITTEN OFFERS

You've done all your homework, marketed yourself, visited colleges and you are sitting in a college coaches office and he/she gives you an athletic financial aid "verbal offer" to be a member of his/her team – what does it mean?

First, confirm that the coach has actually given you an official financial scholarship "verbal offer." So many times, we've heard that a prospective student-athlete comes away feeling they have an offer at hand, and no offer was extended. Often coaches will discuss the possibility of what an offer *might* consist of, *if* he/she decided on you as a team member. If the coach doesn't preface his/her discussion regarding scholarship money with, "this is not an official offer" and you are unsure, then simply ask. There is nothing inappropriate in asking, especially if the coach has broached the subject of a possible scholarship offer.

Once you are certain that a coach has extended a scholarship "verbal offer," express your appreciation. And, if he/she doesn't advise you that he/she will be sending you a written offer to follow up, then ask if you will be receiving the information in writing. ALWAYS request an offer in writing. However, *if you have not begun your junior year in high school (September 1), the coach does not have the ability to send anything in writing except questionnaires and camp brochures.*

According to NCAA Division I regulations: College coaches may *not* **contact you in person, or by telephone, off their campus, until July 1 (or June 15 for Division II) after your junior year. They may ONLY send you questionnaires and camp brochures beginning your freshman and sophomore years; and may send you printed recruiting materials beginning September 1 of your junior year.**

Thank the coach and let him/her know that you would like some time to think about it, and discuss it with your parents. Do not make a decision right there on the spot. This is a big decision and you need time to digest and discuss all of the information presented to you. Be informed; ask questions about your offer:

- What exactly is the amount being offered? (some coaches will give you a dollar amount and other's will give you a percentage; *confirm the dollar amount*)
- Is your offer based on in-state or out-of-state fees? (if you are an out-of-state student applying at a public university, this is a very important question)
- When will I receive a written offer?
- Do I have the ability to earn a larger scholarship as the year's progress?
- What athletic requirements must I satisfy to maintain my scholarship?
- How many credits do I need to maintain my athletic scholarship?
- Is there a minimum GPA required to keep my scholarship?

* Am I eligible for other financial aid? (i.e. academic, non-repayable government aid, etc.)

If accepted, an athletic scholarship amount is only valid for the first year of college, having to be renewed by the student and the college each year thereafter. Therefore, don't assume that your offer is good for the full four years. Work hard and prove your worth on the team each year, and it is likely you will remain on an athletic scholarship.

If a coach offers you a scholarship amount for the first year and states that he/she will offer more the following three years, this is not a guarantee. An offer is on a per year basis. We've spoken to students and parents who specifically chose a school based on a coach's pledge for higher scholarship money for the following years, which never came to pass due to budget constraints or other reasons; leaving the student without anticipated funds for their upper class college years.

Neither a "verbal" offer nor a "written" offer is a legally binding agreement. Until the National Letter of Intent is signed, at any time either you or the coach can rescind his/her offer or your acceptance.

As we've state earlier, it is uncommon to have a coach rescind an offer, however, much more common for prospective student-athletes to withdraw from a verbal commitment, for one reason or another. Coaches are constantly recruiting and have likely been through this process many times, they are very particular in their decisions. Additionally, a coach values their reputation and if he/she recants an offer, it can become quite controversial. That being said, a coach has every right, and should, rescind an offer if the student-athlete violates a rule or behaves in a manner that is unsuitable to the team or university. Generally speaking, you can consider a coach's scholarship offer as reliable.

While an offer is commonly extended from a coach, it is really an offer from the institution. Should the coach leave the institution before you begin your freshman year (or later if you are a transfer student), the offer should still be in place. As a courtesy, the coach should notify you of his/her departure, but if he/she does not, check with the Athletic Director to confirm your offer is still in place.

Keeping all correspondence relevant to your chosen institution is imperative. Keep all emails and letters from the coach and the institution, for your records.

Once an offer is extended to you, it is your responsibility to decline or accept the offer. A coach will definitely want a verbal "accept" or "decline" before the signing dates.

Whether you are accepting or declining a coach's offer, a phone call is the most professional way to communicate your decision to the coach, and shows a lot of character. Remember, coaches' talk, and you want to leave each one feeling that you are an admirable student who deserves the best. If declining, always complement the coach's institution and/or program and thank them for their time. If you must email or write, do so in the same manner.

A sample "decline" email is below:

> To: coachb@xyzu.edu
> From: student@home.com
>
> Hi Coach B:
>
> I want to thank you for your kind offer to join XYZ University's golf team. After much deliberation, I find it necessary to decline your offer.
>
> My parents and I very much enjoyed the time we spent with you and the team members on campus. XYZ University is a wonderful college, and has a great deal to offer students. You have a terrific golf program and I wish you all the best in your upcoming season.
>
> Again, thank you for all of your time and effort.
>
> Sincerely,
>
> Your name
> Your cell phone number
> Your email address

FINANCES

We would never presume to completely understand *all* the in's and out's of the multitude of scholarships, foundations, and money out there to help a student pay for college. It is a web of rules, regulations, and arbitrary determinations that, at times, seem to have no meaning at all. In the end, with college costs at an astronomical level and skyrocketing further every year, students and their families need assistance.

Generally speaking, financial aid comes in different forms; typically, they are academic, athletic, need-based, minority based, and family or legacy. We have provided some general information regarding federal, local, and college based financial aid. However, our absolute best advice on financial aid, is to check with your high school counselor, speak with the financial aid officer at your potential college (they are extremely knowledgeable about financial aid packages), and/or research the internet and books on the subject.

We briefly touched on academic financial aid from colleges in the section on **"Applying to Colleges."** In essence, most institutions offer academic scholarships on a per school basis. Each school has their own system for scholarship acceptance. Most colleges that offer academic scholarships use a calculation of your GPA, SAT, and/or ACT compared with their existing incoming freshman applications. Other schools may use a more standardized ladder approach utilizing GPA, SAT, and/or ACT scores, without comparing these scores to incoming freshman acceptances. Always check with the college by checking their website and calling the financial aid officer at that particular institution.

College athletic scholarships are awarded based on the amount a coach is physically allowed to offer from his/her institution and his/her governing organization, divided by his/her team members. A full scholarship is defined as the cost of tuition, fees, room, board, and books.

Golf is known as an "equivalency sport" (according to the NCAA) and the coach has the ability to divide his/her allotted scholarship amounts as he/she sees fit among team members. This gives the coach the opportunity to use a variety of different percentages based on their assessment of each player's stature on the team. It is difficult to be granted a full ride in an "equivalency sport."

Each governing organization and division allows a certain maximum amount of scholarships for their college golf teams. Below is a table showing the scholarship allowances by division. Bear in mind that some schools, no matter what division, are not fully funded – ask the coach if the golf program is fully funded, and how many scholarships he/she has at his/her disposal.

GOLF SCHOLARSHIP MAXIMUM ALLOWANCES

Organization	Men	Women
NCAA Division I	4.5 Scholarships	6.0 Scholarships
NCAA Division II	3.6 Scholarships	5.4 Scholarships
NCAA Division III	No Athletic Scholarships	No Athletic Scholarships
NAIA	5 Scholarships	5 Scholarships
NJCAA Division I	8 Scholarships	8 Full/Partial Scholarships
NJCAA Division II	8 Partial Scholarships	N/A
NJCAA Division III	No Athletic Scholarships	N/A

Need-based federal financial aid is a calculated amount, based on your family's finances, dependencies, and college costs. The Free Application for Student Aid (FAFSA) has become the standard by which federal aid is calculated. Often, schools and states offer their own form of need-based aid, using the FAFSA calculations.

Federal aid is awarded to students in the form of grants, student loans, and work-study programs. It is definitely worth exploring the

FAFSA website and completing their worksheet, even if you don't believe you qualify (www.fafsa.ed.gov). You might be pleasantly surprised with the results. The financial aid officer at your potential college is your best resource to understanding FAFSA, and other need-based financial aid resources (they are experts on financial aid). They might have a simple assessment form for you to complete, which they can use to evaluate your possible FAFSA contributions.

Additionally, there are varieties of private, public, and local scholarships available. Check with your high school counselor, college career center, search the web, and books. Each year, financial aid money goes unused by students because of a lack of research. Many students don't want to go to the effort of applying, and possibly writing essays, for $500 or $1,000; but remember that it all adds up.

Typically, you are able to combine athletic scholarships, academic scholarships, outside grants, and financial aid funds to pay for college costs. Check with your potential college financial aid officer to determine what combination is permitted by their institution. They will work with you to combine the funds properly to create a complete financial aid package, which is in your best interest.

THE FINAL DECISION

If you've only been extended one offer and you are confident this is the place for you, then your final decision is a simple one. However, it is more likely that after all of your efforts, you will be faced with choosing between two or more schools and golf programs. This is the time to sit down with a pen, paper, and your parents. Remember, it is rare that one institution has it *all*.

Make a list of the pros and cons of each school based on their academics, golf program, financial awards, location, proximity, look and feel. Pull out your notes and photos from your visits to compare, and ask and answer questions for each school. You may even want to come up with a system to rate your answers for each school (i.e. bad, good, very good, great or 1-5 with 1 being bad and 5 being fantastic).

Golf

- How do I like the coach?
- How do I like the team members?
- Do I feel I fit well with the team members?
- How do I like the golf facilities?
- Do I like the practice courses?
- Do they have decent indoor facilities?
- What do I think of their golf schedule?
- How do I like the workout facilities?
- What are my thoughts on the golf program's ranking? Does it fit me?
- What is the history of their program – long established or newer?
- Where do I feel I fit in amongst the team?
- Will I immediately be in the top five travel players?
- How often do I feel I will play in tournaments?
- What is the general weather like at this location for playing golf?
- What is my overall opinion of this school's golf program?

Academic

- Do they have my academic major?
- Is it the teacher/student ratio I am looking for?
- Are their academic programs well rated?
- Do their education requirements fit me as an overall student?
- Do I feel their academics would be either too easy or too hard?

Financial

- What will we be paying at each institution once all of my aid is added up against the total tuition, fees, room, board, and books?
- Am I happy with the financial aid package I received?

Campus

- Is it the right population size and layout for me?
- Is it in a location I am happy with?
- Was I impressed with the classroom set up and modernization?
- Which buildings was I very impressed with?
- Which buildings was I not so impressed with?

- Which buildings are the most important to me?
- What do I like or dislike about the surrounding area?
- Does it have the look and feel I am searching for?

Once you've answered all of your questions, really evaluate everything with your parents. Look over your notes and photos to refresh your memory, and go back and forth. Remember your visit(s), and visualize what you liked and didn't like about each institution. Above all, take your time.

The coaches may ask when you will have your decision and they may continue to contact you to check on your selection. Let them know in a kind, mature manner that you are weighing your decision carefully between two (or however many) offers (no need to tell them which schools), and are looking to have your final decision by XXX (give them a day or date). Again, be very complimentary of them, their program, their team, and the institution – after all, you will be attending one of these schools.

An email like this is appropriate:

To: coachb@xyzu.edu
From: student@home.com

Hi Coach B:

Thank you for your offer and continued contact. My parent(s) and I thoroughly enjoyed our time with you and the team members at XYZ University. You have an excellent golf program and exemplary academics. I was particularly impressed with your golf facilities, style of team management, student union, and library *[list a few things about each part of your visit that impressed you]*.

I am weighing my decision carefully, and hope to make a final choice by next Wednesday. I hope this is convenient for you.

We really appreciate all of the time and effort you put into our fantastic visit. Again, thank you, and feel free to contact me anytime.

Sincerely,

THE FINAL DECISION

Giving the coach a timeframe also helps motivate you to finalize your choice. At this stage, once you have carefully reviewed your pros and cons list, and discussed it with your parents, your choice should be clear. It may be a tough one, and there may be two schools that are virtually equal on your list, but there will always be a few items that stand out about one particular institution and/or golf program.

SIGNING – THE NATIONAL LETTER OF INTENT

You've decided and accepted the verbal/written offer to the college of your choice! Once you've accepted a "verbal offer," the NCAA Division I or Division II institution will send you a **National Letter of Intent** package just prior to the official signing dates. You will want to carefully review your package before you sign the agreement(s). (Division III, NAIA, and NJCAA do not participate in the NLI – NAIA and NJCAA have their own Letter of Intent)

> **The NCAA National Letter of Intent early signing period for golf usually begins the second Wednesday in November and runs for eight days. The regular National Letter of Intent signing period usually begins in mid-April and runs to early August. Check www.nationalletter.org for the exact dates.**

The National Letter of Intent is a binding agreement between the student-athlete and the institution, where the student-athlete agrees to attend the institution for *one academic* year and the institution agrees to provide athletic financial aid for *one academic* year. Athletic scholarships are renewable each year at the coach's discretion. The coach and/or athletic director notify the student-athlete each year of his/her athletic financial aid for the upcoming year, and the NLI does not need to be signed each year. The NLI is still binding even if the coach departs from the college. You are signing an agreement with the institution, not the coach.

In your package, you will receive the National Letter of Intent and an Athletics Financial Aid Agreement. You must sign two copies of both documents along with your parent or legal guardian (if you are under 21), and send one copy back to the institution.

Once signed and returned, you are bound to this institution for *one academic* year and all other institutions must cease any recruiting efforts towards you, until you are enrolled in the college. After enrollment, new recruiting regulations go into effect under the NCAA guidelines. Should you choose not to attend this school, there is a Release Request and an Appeal Process, which you will need to file. More than likely, a penalty will be imposed for not fulfilling your contract. (Download the "A Quick Reference Guide to the NLI" for information pertaining to the NLI and check the NLI regulations at www.nationalletter.org)

Basic Information on signing the National Letter of Intent and the Athletics Financial Aid Agreement:

* Sign two copies of the National Letter of Intent and Athletics Financial Aid Agreement from the institution.
* Your parent or legal guardian must also sign if you are under 21.
* The documents must be signed together and not before the official golf signing periods as stated by the NCAA.
* The documents must be signed within 14 days of the date they were issued.
* Return one copy back to the institution.
* The Athletics Financial Aid Agreement must include the student-athlete's NCAA ID number provided by the NCAA Eligibility Center upon registration.
* Your potential college coach, at that institution, cannot be present at the signing.
* Once signed, you must fulfill your agreement to attend one full *academic* year at that institution.
* All other institutions attempting to recruit you must cease all recruiting efforts.

At the end of Chapter One, we presented a series of questions for you to ask yourself prior to signing a National Letter of Intent. It is imperative that you are sure you are making the right decision. This is one of the most important decisions you will make at your age, and an NLI is a binding agreement. At the risk of sounding overly redundant, we feel it pertinent to re-list those same

SIGNING–NATIONAL LETTER OF INTENT

questions again, to reiterate the importance of knowing before you sign.

Questions Before You Sign

* **Are you proud to say I attend XYZ University?**
  You will know if you are settling if you aren't proud of your university and shouting it from the rooftops. Take some time to really visualize yourself at that university, with the team, and with the coach.

* **Are you comfortable with the size and educational offerings at the college?**
  If this is not the school size you are really comfortable in, or it doesn't offer the major you would like, then this is not the place for you. You should get a good idea of these aspects when you are visiting the school. If it feels too cramped or too overwhelming, then you need to keep looking to find the right feel and educational offerings for you.

* **Are you comfortable with the coach and team members?**
  These ten to fifteen people are your new family for the next four years. Make certain you are comfortable with them, and can see yourself working and living with them over the years.

* **Are you comfortable with the level of golf this team projects?**
  If they don't have the same level of golf life style and attitude you do, then this is not the school for you. You may want to see more or less dedication, organization, commitment, and drive – if it's not right on par with who you are and what you are looking for, then keep going on your pursuit.

* **Do you feel you are on par academically and can keep your grades up in this environment?**
  If you feel you may really be reaching to maintain a good solid GPA at this school, it is more than likely not for you. College is a huge adjustment from high school and much more demanding. When you compound this transition with the additional pressure of traveling on a collegiate sport's team, it becomes even more stressful. Most college teams pride

themselves on their team's GPA, which adds another level of demands on you. Make sure your academic abilities are a good fit.

* ***Does this school have the look and feel for you?***
  This may sound a bit intangible, but it is what your first impression of a school is always about. If it's not what you envisioned; too small, too large, too spread out, too cramped together, too modern, too old, etc., then this is not where you'll be comfortable.

This is a very happy time for the student-athlete, their families, their high school coach, and their college coach. Commonly, the signing is held at the high school, with your high school coach and family, with pictures and your name in the paper, culminating in a celebration with cake and friends. Your athletic and academic accomplishments, and marketing efforts have paid off; you are about to attend a wonderful college and play on a college golf team!

Congratulations!

QUESTIONS TO ASK BEFORE YOU SIGN

www.ACollegeGolfPlan.com

Chapter 8

Know the Governing Organizations

As we've noted, throughout this book we have written mostly with NCAA Division I and II rules in mind. However, there are other governing organizations with their own specific requirements, which also offer outstanding college golf opportunities.

Regardless, all of the athletic governing organizations have two general goals in mind and they are, to protect the prospective student-athlete from unfair and inequitable recruiting tactics and to integrate intercollegiate athletics into higher education. These governing agencies also provide guidelines, compliance officers, and committees for prospective and collegiate student-athletes to approach should they feel they have been treated in an unfair manner. In essence, the NCAA, NAIA, and NJCAA are there to protect you, the student-athlete. They promote education, athletics, fair play, sportsmanlike conduct, spirit, and community.

NCAA

There are three Divisions in the National Collegiate Athletic Association (NCAA). Division I typically contains the highest athletically performing member institutions, followed closely by Division II and Division III. All Divisions have excellent member colleges, which afford superior educational programs and opportunities. When searching for colleges, don't rule out any of these divisions; they all offer competitive athletics and exemplary educational curriculums. The NCAA website at www.ncaa.org provides in depth information about their organization.

Before beginning the recruiting process, you should download the "NCAA Guide for the College-Bound Student-Athlete" at www.ncaastudent.org. This guide is an invaluable resource for prospective student-athletes. It provides a wealth of information about the NCAA rules and guidelines on how to proceed in your recruiting process. The guide walks you through the requirements for playing collegiate golf in the NCAA. When reviewing the recruiting rules on the NCAA websites, men's and women's golf falls under the category of "all other sports."

While it would be nearly impossible for you to know all of the NCAA rules, it is still your responsibility to be generally aware of the requirements during your college search. You should know when you or a coach may be in violation of a rule, and ask. If serious enough, violations only hurt you and can prevent you from playing at any NCAA school for a full year. The NCAA student guide is an excellent resource to begin your education.

Generally speaking, NCAA Division I and II schools have similar recruiting rules with subtle nuances. Division III, however, has a separate set of guidelines and Division III colleges are not permitted to offer athletic scholarships. There are NCAA rules interspersed throughout this book that we feel are relevant to the topic being discussed, on that page. In this section, we have provided you with a table of general recruiting rules and timelines for NCAA Division I, II, and III. Again, always research, and ask, if you have a question about a rule. College coaches are required to stay abreast of NCAA guidelines and should know the rules; and if it is questionable, the on-campus compliance officer can help with understanding certain restrictions.

NCAA SUMMARY OF GOLF RECRUITING RULES

	Division I	Division II	Division III
Freshman/Sophomore Year	**Recruiting Materials:** May receive camp brochures and questionnaires.	**Recruiting Materials:** May receive camp brochures and questionnaires.	**Recruiting Materials:** May receive any printed materials.
	Telephone Calls: • You may make calls to the coach at your expense only. • College coach cannot call you.	**Telephone Calls:** • You may make calls to the coach at your expense only. • College coach cannot call you.	**Telephone Calls:** No limitations on calls to/from you and the college coach.
	Off-campus contact: None allowed	**Off-campus contact:** None allowed	**Off-campus contact:** None allowed
	Unofficial Visit: You may make an unlimited number of unofficial visits.	**Unofficial Visit:** You may make an unlimited number of unofficial visits.	**Unofficial Visit:** You may make an unlimited number of unofficial visits.
	Official Visit: None allowed	**Official Visit:** None allowed	**Official Visit:** None allowed

NCAA GUIDELINES

	Division I	Division II	Division III
Junior Year	**Recruiting Materials:** You may begin receiving printed recruiting materials on September 1 of your Junior Year. **Telephone Calls:** • You may make calls to the coach at your expense. • A College coach may call you once per week starting July 1 after your Junior Year. **Off-campus contact:** Allowed starting July 1 after your junior year. **Unofficial Visit:** You may make an unlimited number of unofficial visits. **Official Visit:** None allowed.	**Recruiting Materials:** You may begin receiving printed recruiting materials on September 1 of your Junior Year. **Telephone Calls:** • You may make calls to the coach at your expense. • A College coach may call you once per week starting June 15 after your Junior Year. **Off-campus contact:** Allowed starting June 15 after your junior year. **Unofficial Visit:** You may make an unlimited number of unofficial visits. **Official Visit:** None Allowed.	**Recruiting Materials:** May receive any printed materials. **Telephone Calls:** No limitations on call to/from you and the coach. **Off-campus contact:** Allowed immediately after the end of your junior year. **Unofficial Visit:** You may make an unlimited number of unofficial visits. **Official Visit:** None allowed

	Division I	Division II	Division III
Senior Year	**Recruiting Materials:** You may begin receiving printed recruiting materials on September 1 of your Junior Year. **Telephone Calls:** ● You may make calls to the coach at your expense. ● A College coach may call you once per week starting July 1 after your Junior Year. **Off-campus contact:** Allowed starting July 1 after your junior year. **Official Visit:** ● Allowed beginning opening day of your senior year classes. ● You are limited to one official visit per college up to a maximum of five separate colleges. **Unofficial Visit:** You may make an unlimited number of unofficial visits. **Evaluations and Contacts:** Up to seven times during your senior year.	**Recruiting Materials:** You may begin receiving printed recruiting materials on September 1 of your Junior Year. **Telephone Calls:** ● You may make calls to the coach at your expense. ● A College coach may call you once per week starting June 15 after your Junior Year. **Off-campus contact:** Allowed starting June 15 after your junior year. **Official Visit:** ● Allowed beginning opening day of your senior year classes. ● You are limited to one official visit per college up to a maximum of five separate colleges. **Unofficial Visit:** You may make an unlimited number of unofficial visits.	**Recruiting Materials:** May receive any printed materials. **Telephone Calls:** No limitations on call to/from you and the coach. **Off-campus contact:** Allowed immediately after the end of your junior year. **Official Visit:** ● Allowed beginning opening day of your senior year classes. ● You are limited to one official visit per college. **Unofficial Visit:** You may make an unlimited number of unofficial visits.

NCAA GUIDELINES

NCAA ELIGIBILITY CENTER

Playing in NCAA Division I or II means you must be certified as an amateur student-athlete. In the beginning of your junior year, you must register with the NCAA Eligibility Center and complete all of the steps and information required at www.eligibilitycenter.org, to prove your amateur status and be eligible to play NCAA sports.

You must also send them a sealed copy of your transcripts, your SAT, and ACT scores. When sending your SAT and ACT scores electronically, the Eligibility Center's code is 9999 (send SATs from www.collegeboard.com and send ACTs from www.actstudent.org). Check with your high school counselor on the proper procedures for sending your high school transcripts. If your high school does not send transcripts electronically, it may be up to you to send a sealed copy to the Eligibility Center. (Check the website at www.eligibilitycenter.org for the mailing address)

Additionally, you must graduate on time (in eight semesters) with your incoming freshman class and satisfy the Division I or II Core Course requirements. These requirements are further explained in the "NCAA Guide for the College-Bound Student-Athlete" at www.ncaastudent.org.

There are six sections to completing the Eligibility Center information, which include:

Create An Account/Register:
When completing your email address, make sure it is a valid email address, which you will maintain throughout your high school years. Your email address will also become your username.

About Me:
This section asks general questions about your name, date of birth, gender, address, and contact information.

Coursework:

This section asks you to enter all high schools you have attended during your high school years and answer a few simple questions about the type of classes you've taken.

My Sports:

You will choose your sport and answer questions regarding any financial awards you may have received during your playing years. This is where you prove your amateur status for your sport.

> **Once you have completed the above sections and sent your payment, you will receive a userid (your email address), password, and an NCAA ID number.**

Once you've registered, the following sections will be revealed on the front page of your "My Planner" section.

My Transcripts:

Send a sealed copy of your transcripts. This area will show if they have received your transcripts. There are lines with your High School(s) name(s), and a line with "Final Transcript/Proof of Graduation." Once your transcripts are received by the Eligibility Center, a check will appear in the checkbox next to your High School(s) name(s).

Check with your high school guidance counselor on their procedures for sending your final transcript and proof of graduation after you have completed your senior year. This is an important part of the process. You must receive certification of amateur status from the Eligibility Center before your freshman year of college to play golf and accept your athletic financial award. You will receive your certificate after the Eligibility Center receives your final transcripts, your proof of graduation, and all other areas are satisfied.

NCAA ELIGIBILITY CENTER

My Test Scores:
Send your ACT and SAT scores. Again, there are two lines in this area which indicate whether your ACT and SAT scores have been received by a check or no check in the check box area.

NAIA

The National Association of Intercollegiate Athletics (NAIA) is the athletic governing organization of nearly 300 member institutions. The NAIA has been an athletic governing body for over 70 years and is divided into 25 conferences, offers 13 sports and 23 championships. It boasts that more than 90% of their member schools offer athletic scholarships. They are dedicated to promoting academic excellence and development, through athletic participation.

NAIA Membership schools are mostly comprised of college's with smaller populations, which can be very beneficial both athletically and academically. The athletics are very competitive, with maximum playing time opportunities for athletes.

The NAIA has it's own recruiting requirements, amateur status requirements, eligibility center and more. They offer fewer recruiting restrictions with more contact between student-athletes and college coaches. To find out more about the NAIA visit their website at www.naia.org or http://naia.cstv.com/member-services, or call them at 816.595.8000.

NJCAA

The National Junior College Athletic Association (NJCAA) is the athletics governing organization for two-year colleges (junior colleges). The NJCAA is it's own governing organization and has it's own recruiting requirements, amateur status requirements, eligibility affidavit and letter of intent. Member colleges of the NJCAA Division I and II typically offer athletic scholarships.

The NJCAA provides students with an excellent opportunity to play very competitive collegiate golf while receiving an Associates Degree, studying for a Certificate Program, or pursuing their four-year core courses prior to completing their Bachelor's Degree at a four-year institution. Junior collegiate golf follows a similar competitive schedule to the four-year institutions, and is very well ranked within college athletics.

The best place to receive information and documentation regarding the NJCAA is, www.njcaa.org/todaysNJCAA.cfm or call them at 719.590.9788. Their website provides you with all of the necessary rules and forms to participate in college golf at a Junior College.

NAIA AND NJCAA

www.ACollegeGolfPlan.com

GLOSSARY OF TERMS

Contact: An off-campus face-to-face contact with you or your parents and a college coach.

Contact Period: A college coach can have in-person contact with you or your parents on or off campus.

Dead Period: A college coach cannot have any in-person contact with you or your parents on or off campus. For golf, this period is commonly during early signing days in November and the first week of signing days in mid-April.

Evaluation: Any off-campus activity designed by a coach to evaluate your academic or athletics ability.

Evaluation Period: A college coach may watch you play, but cannot have conversations with you or your parents off the college's campus.

National Letter of Intent (NLI): A voluntary program administered by the Eligibility Center. The NLI is a binding agreement between the institution and the prospective student-athlete.

Official Visit: Any visit to a college campus by you and your parents, partially or fully paid for by the college.

Prospective Student Athlete: Any student-athlete who has begun the ninth grade.

Redshirt: A collegiate student-athlete who practices but does not compete against outside competition for one academic year. You have not used a season of competition and are allowed a total of four seasons of competition.

Quiet Period: A college coach cannot have any in-person contact with you or your parents off campus.

Unofficial Visit: Any visit to a college campus by you and your parents paid for by you and/or your parents.

Verbal Commitment: A student-athlete's pledge to the coach that he/she intends to accept their scholarship offer and attend their institution prior to signing the National Letter of Intent.

RESOURCES

Academic Web Sites

ACT: *www.actstudent.org*

College Board: *www.collegeboard.com*

Free Application for Student Aid (FAFSA): *www.fafsa.ed.gov*

Athletic Organizations

National Collegiate Athletic Assoc (NCAA): *www.ncaa.org*

NCAA Student Site: *www.ncaastudent.org*

NCAA Eligibility Center: *www.eligibilitycenter.org*

NAIA: *www.naia.org*
(National Association of Intercollegiate Athletics)

NJCAA: *www.njcaa.org*
(National Junior College Athletic Association)

National Letter of Intent (NLI): *www.nationalletter.org*

Golf Web Sites

American Junior Golf Association (AJGA): *www.ajga.org*

College Golf Combines: *www.collegegolfcombines.com*

Future Collegians World Tour (FCWT): *www.fcwtgolf.com*

Golf Handicap & Information Network (GHIN): *www.ghin.com*

Golfstat: *www.golfstat.com*

Golfweek: *www.golfweek.com*

International Junior Golf Tour (IJGT): *www.ijgt.com*

National Junior Golf Scoreboard: *www.njgs.com*

Optimist Junior Golf: *www.optimist.org*

Golf Web Sites

Professional Golf Association (PGA): *www.pga.com*

PGA Junior Series: *www.pgajuniorseries.com*

Southern Golf Association: *www.sgagolf.com*

U.S. Golf Association: *www.usga.org*

Western Golf Association: *www.westerngolfassociation.com*

ABOUT THE AUTHOR

Amy Bodin has supported heads of Fortune 500 companies, worked with high profile news reporters, spearheaded multifaceted marketing campaigns, designed and compiled intricate sales and marketing research data worldwide, and assisted in copyediting of several published works over the past 25 years.

One of her greatest challenges came when faced with the daunting task of helping her son realize his dream of playing college golf. Astonished by the complex nature of college golf recruiting, and the mind-boggling lack of cohesive information out there for the junior golfer and their parents; she set out to develop a logical system to traverse the complicated world of college golf recruiting. Drawing from her vast research, marketing, and copyediting experience, she designed A College Golf Plan for *every* junior golfer, and their parents.

She lives in Texas with her husband and three children.

ACollegeGolfPlan.com

Please visit our website at www.ACollegeGolfPlan.com for more information, services, and links. We would love to hear your comments, suggestions, and testimonials.

CPSIA information can be obtained at www.ICGtesting.com
Printed in the USA
BVOW031406191211

278730BV00007B/104/P